	Page	CD Track
Live Performance	69	
Latin	69	46

M

	Page	CD Track
Meter	71	
Maintenance	71	
March	72	47
Motown	72	48
Mambo	74	49
MIDI	74	
Microphones	75	

N

	Page	CD Track
Nanigo	77	50

O

	Page	CD Track
Odd Meters	78	51–52
Ostinato	81	53
Over and Through the Bar Line	82	54
Overdub	82	55

P

	Page	CD Track
Practice	84	
Play-along	84	56
Programming	87	57
Pro Tools	87	
Punk	87	58
Pedals (Bass Drum and Hi-hat)	89	

Q

	Page	CD Track
Quarter-note Grooves	90	59–60

R

	Page	CD Track
Reading	91	
Rudiments	92	61-62
Ride Cymbal	94	63
Repetition	95	
Road	95	
Rhythmic Guide	96	64
Reggae	98	65
Rock	98	66
Rest	100	
Rhythm Section	101	67

S

	Page	CD Track
Snare Drum	102	68
Snare Wires	103	
Sticks	103	
Speed	104	
Studio Tips	105	
Sequenced Grooves	106	69–70
Swing Feel	106	71
Samba	107	72
Shuffle	108	73
Second Line (New Orleans)	109	74
Subbing	110	
Solo	110	75
Syncopation	112	

T

	Page	CD Track
Tempo	113	
Tom-Tom	113	76
Tambourine	114	77
Tuning	114	78
Technique	115	
Time (time-feel)	116	

U

	Page	CD Track
Universal Language	117	

V

	Page	CD Track
Volume	118	
Vocalize	118	

W

	Page	CD Track
World Music	119	79–80
Waltz	120	81

X

	Page	CD Track
X-ray	122	

Y

	Page	CD Track
Yield	123	

Z

	Page	CD Track
Zoom	124	
Zany Grooves and Fills	124	82

786.9193
R791s

FOREWORD
by Joe Porcaro

Ed's *Stuff! Good Drummers Should Know* book/CD is a wealth of information for the drummer and percussionist who aims to reach the next performance level. It is a valuable resource that will benefit those drummers early in their careers as well as the professional, working musician. This CD package is a must, as Ed's performances will inspire and help you attain your goals. His concepts and down to earth stories are priceless. Ed will keep you engaged and listening, and will arm you with the tools to succeed in today's music business.

ABOUT THE AUTHOR

Ed Roscetti, originally from New York City, is a drummer, composer, educator, author, and clinician. His critically praised Hal Leonard publications include *Drummer's Guide to Odd Meters*; *Blues Drumming*; *Funk & Hip-Hop Drumming*; *Rock Drumming Workbook*; and the *World Beat Rhythms Series: Brazil*, *Africa*, and *Cuba*. He has been a core curriculum author for twenty-five years at The Musicians Institute's Percussion Institute of Technology (PIT), and conducts concerts, clinics, workshops, and music camps across the country.

Roscetti has performed, produced, and composed for numerous records, TV shows, and films, such as *Saturday Night Live*, *The 60's*, The History Channel, WWE, *General Hospital*, and *Santa Barbara*, and has worked with Quincy Jones, Herbie Hancock, Joe Sample, the Crusaders, Benny Golson, Gary Wright, Tommy Tedesco, Joe Porcaro, and Jeff Porcaro, among others.

Ed endorses the following companies: Drum Workshop/Pacific, Paiste, Remo, Regal Tip, Shure Inc., Drum Tech, Puresound, and E-pad.

Professional Affiliations:

American Society of Composers, Authors and Publishers (ASCAP)

National Academy of Recording Arts and Sciences (NARAS)

American Federation of Musicians (AFM)

Society of Composers and Lyricists (SCL)

Percussive Arts Society (PAS)

International Association for Jazz Education (IAJE)

You may correspond with Ed Roscetti at **allmusic@roscettimusic.com**, or visit his websites at **www.roscettimusic.com** and **www.worldbeatrhythms.com**.

ACKNOWLEDGMENTS

Special thanks to:

Claudia Dunn; Sebastian Aymanns; Joe Porcaro; Jeff Stern; Damon Tedesco; Pathik Desai; David Hughes; Silvio Bruno; Alan V; Maria Martinez; John Snider; Fred Dinkins; Ryan Poyer; Louie Marino; my loving partner Claudia and my family, Armeto, Ann, and Linda Roscetti, Roscetti Music; and World Beat Rhythms.

Thanks for your support:

Scott Donnell, Juels Thomas, Garrison, Don Lombardi and John Good at Drum Workshop/ Pacific; Andrew Shreve, Ed Clift, and Tim Shahady at Paiste; Carol Calato and Cathy Calato at Regal Tip; Bruce Jacoby, Matt Connors, Chris Hart, and Brock Kaericher at Remo; Ryan Smith at Shure, Inc.; Yoav and Jeff Stern at Puresound; Chandra Lynn at DigiDesign; Tom Henry at Drum Tech; and Jeff Schroedl and Bruce Bush at Hal Leonard Corporation.

Ed Roscetti uses the following equipment:

DW and Pacific Drums (Drum Workshop/Pacific)—dwdrums.com, www.pacificdrums.com

Paiste Cymbals and Gongs—www.paiste.com

Remo Drum Heads and World Percussion (Remo)—www.remo.com

Regal Tip Sticks, Brushes, and Mallets (Regal Tip)—www.regaltip.com

KSM 32's, 44's, KSM 27's, and Beta Series Microphones (Shure, Inc.)—www.shure.com

Pro Tools LE (003) and HD systems (DigiDesign)—www.digidesign.com

Digimax Mic Pre (PreSonus)—www.presonus.com

DTS Tuning System (Drum Tech)—www.drumtech.com

Puresound Snare Wires (Puresound)—www.puresoundpercussion.com

Dedication:

This book is dedicated to my family: Claudia, Linda, Armeto, and Ann.

INTRODUCTION

Stuff! Good Drummers Should Know is an A to Z encyclopedia of my best 119 tips, including an 82-track performance CD. These pieces of advice have either been passed down from those who went before me, or hard-earned through that age-old teacher, personal experience. Many of the tips are self-contained, while others include examples that will ask you to reference additional tips within the book. The basic grooves are performed on the CD. The beginnings of most examples are written out, though not everything played on the CD is transcribed. At times, you will be asked to finish writing out the rest of a performance. As you work on the individual tips, be sure to write your own grooves, fills, ensemble phrases, and solo ideas in that style. Take every opportunity to get together and play with as many musicians as possible. This will help you to develop your internal clock and time-feel on the drumset. I have made an effort to include a variety of concepts and styles that will help you in your daily pursuit as a working drummer. It is my hope that you enjoy yourself and find something that speaks to you as a musician. If, when finished, you choose to apply even a few of the following concepts to your drumming, then this book/CD has done its job.

Keep groovin'.

Ed Roscetti

ABOUT THE CD

The 82 CD examples are for your listening reference. Some tracks include a rhythm section, others consist of drumset with some percussion, and a few of the tracks are interactive. All performances are not completely written out; tracks that continue beyond the notation have been included for you to hear how certain musical examples might develop over an extended period of time. There are no audio-edit "fixes" on the CD. All drum and percussion parts were cut in real time in the air, or with a click, except for the programmed beats. Many of the tracks include count-off "clicks" so you know when the music will begin. Some tracks have no clicks because it was not necessary for listening purposes.

Credits:

Drums and percussion: Ed Roscetti
Bass: David Hughes
Guitars: Pathik Desai
Keyboards: Ed Roscetti
Additional keyboards: Silvio Bruno
DAW/Studio Tech: Alan V
CD mastering: Damon Tedesco
Drum tech, cartage, additional transcriptions, and Mambo performance
on drumset: Sebastian Aymanns

Recorded, edited, and mixed at Roscetti Music, Studio City, California, by Ed Roscetti and Silvio Bruno, assisted by Sebastian Aymanns

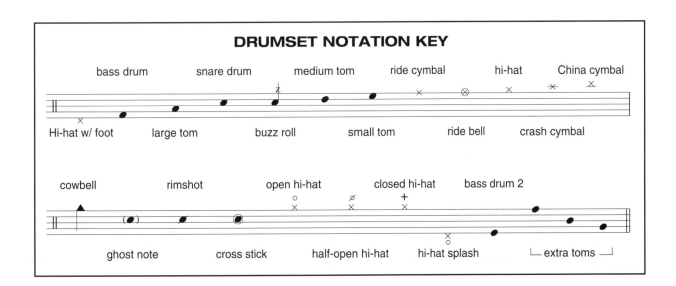

ACCENTS

An *accent* emphasizes or stresses a certain note, chord, or beat, to mark its relative importance in the measure. Accents in rhythm help create forward motion and punctuations in the time-feel and groove. Downbeats and upbeats are the keys to accents. Accents define rhythmic subdivisions within a groove as well as dynamic changes within a phrase. Without accents or forward motion in the rhythm, the groove would feel as if it were standing still.

Play each example below, hand-to-hand against a quarter-note bass drum. Let your body internalize the downbeats, upbeats, and subdivided combinations. Next, write some of your own rhythms with different accent combinations, and practice them.

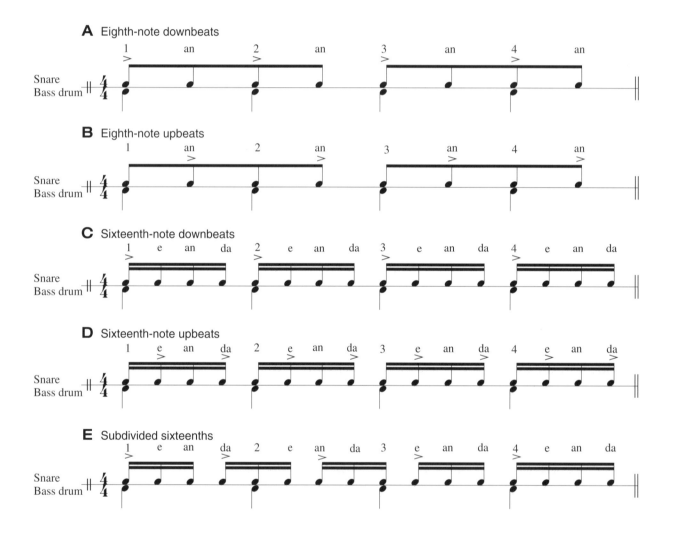

ANTICIPATIONS

Anticipations push the time-feel forward by accenting an upbeat or a downbeat within a musical phrase. Anticipated notes are often short and separated (*staccato*), and played in a crisp, detached style. These notes can also be played as a *tie*, indicated by a curved line joining two notes of the same degree or instrument (i.e., two notes played by the snare drum can be tied together, but a note on the snare drum cannot be tied to a note on the bass drum). In tied notes, the second note is not re-struck, but is simply added on to the duration of the first. A curved line connecting two notes of different degrees or instruments is called a *slur*, and indicates to play the notes in a smooth and connected manner (*legato*), without any break between the tones. This is often used with melodic instruments. In drum charts you will see a combination of both long and short notes within a phrase. Short notes will be played on the snare drum, bass drum, or choked cymbals, and long tones will be played on open hi-hat, bass drum, and crash cymbals. See more on this under *Ensemble Figures* (page 37).

Practice the following examples and then make up your own long and short tones on the drumset. The rhythms are written above the staff as ensemble-figure cues (meaning that these are the rhythms the band would be playing). Orchestrate them around the drumset as you desire.

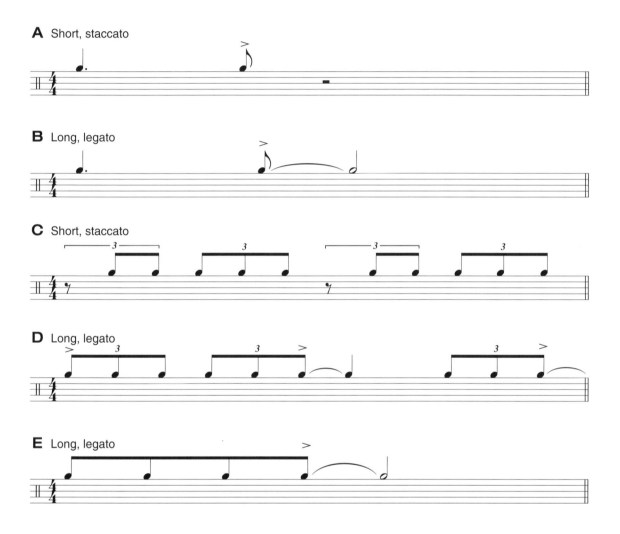

BALANCE

Finding your balance and feeling centered while playing the drumset is very important for your overall performance. The setup, height, and angle of your drums, cymbals, and throne are all factors that contribute to your sense of balance. Sometimes moving your seat, snare drum, cymbal, or toms up or down a few inches will make a huge difference in how you feel when you're playing. Spend time experimenting with your setup. You want to feel comfortable on both the right and left sides of your body (bass drum and hi-hat pedals with the feet, and right and left hands). Try to make your setup flow according to how you play. You don't want to conflict with your time-feel or groove, or waste energy by reaching for toms or cymbals at awkward angles. Though playing the drums is not a sport, it is nonetheless extremely physical. Your setup will become very specific to your body height and weight. You might even change your setup if you have more than one drumset, or if you are playing different styles of music. Remember that the groove comes from the earth—from the ground up through your body—and is centered in your chest area.

The following are a few other tips to try when you are thinking about your balance and setup.

• Never feel like you are reaching for your pedals (i.e., don't sit too high).

• Strive for a feeling of being grounded to the earth, no matter what bass drum or high-hat technique you use.

• Try not to favor the right or left side of your body. Balance out your technique by leading with your left hand or foot if you are right-handed, and the opposite if you are left-handed. This way you'll be feeling both sides of your body while utilizing both sides of your brain.

These will help you to feel more balanced and relaxed behind the drumset. Don't be afraid to try new setups. Changing one thing can open up a whole new approach to your playing.

BRUSHES AND SPECIALTY STICKS

TRACK 1

TRACK 2

As a drummer, you can create a wide variety of sounds with brushes and specialty sticks. CD **Track 1** features a medium-tempo jazz swing feel played on the snare drum with wire brushes. **Track 2** is a medium up-tempo jazz swing feel on the snare drum. See the diagram to the right for hand positions when playing these patterns. You can also use brushes to play the entire drumset, just like using sticks. This is a great sound for softer pop-rock music, and gives you that unplugged sound that blends well with acoustic instruments.

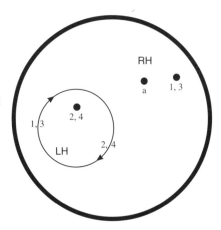

Other specialty sticks such as Blasticks, TyPhoon Sticks, and Thai Sticks can be used to create a wide range of sounds and dynamics. **Track 3** features Blasticks playing a funk groove. Spend some time getting used to playing with different sticks and brushes. You can also mix them up—one drumstick and one brush, or one Blastick and one drumstick—to create different combinations and sounds. It is suggested that you study with a good teacher to work on the traditional style of brush playing.

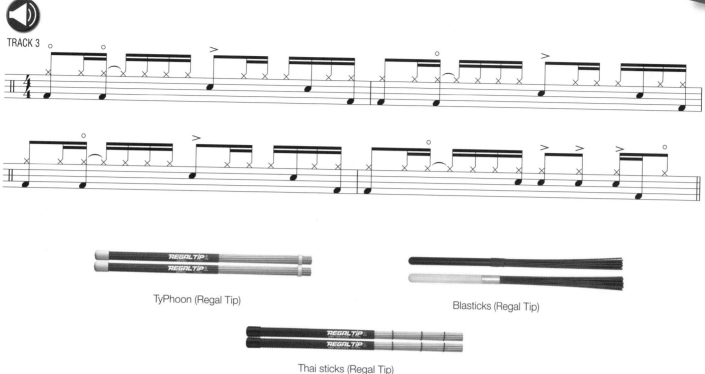

TRACK 3

TyPhoon (Regal Tip)

Blasticks (Regal Tip)

Thai sticks (Regal Tip)

BASS DRUM BEATERS

Materials used to craft beaters can include hard felt, wood, plastic, hard rubber, soft felt, or soft fluff. Some manufacturers offer beaters with more than one option: for example, one side felt and one side hard plastic (good attack for rock, funk, and hip-hop). Others offer large, fluffy beaters, great for recording jazz (depending on the style), or any type of music that isn't too loud. The traditional felt beaters hit a larger area on the bass drum head than do some of the newer felt/plastic beaters. So you need to experiment with different beaters to find the sound you want. When I'm recording, I have a choice of a half-dozen beaters to use, depending on the style of music and/or song. In a live situation, I select a beater that will best comple-ment the music.

DW two-way
beater

DW felt
beater

BLUES

The blues is a melancholic music of black American folk origin. The importance of learn-ing to play the blues cannot be stressed enough. Most all of the great rock, jazz, and R&B musicians across history can play and have been influenced by the blues. The most common blues form that you will run into is the twelve-bar blues. To play the blues, you need to develop a strong swing triplet feel so your shuffle grooves will swing. See *Swing Feel* (p. 106) and *Shuffle* (p. 108) for more on that subject.

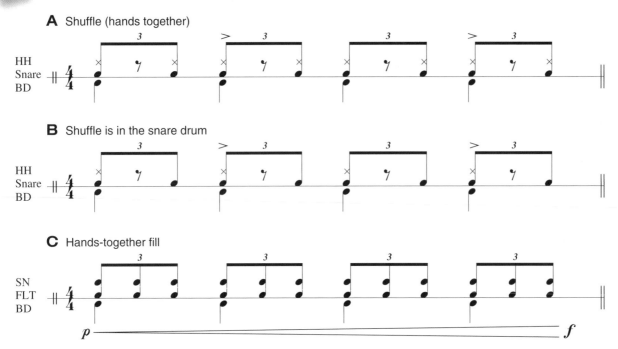

A Shuffle (hands together)

B Shuffle is in the snare drum

C Hands-together fill

Styles can be changed drastically and plugged into a blues song form. Spend time listening to the other instruments in the ensemble—bass, piano, guitar, vocals, and horns—so you can train your ears to hear the chord changes in a blues form. This will help tell you where you are in the form of the song. The less commonly used blues form—the eight-bar blues (see chart below)—is sometimes used in rock 'n' roll. In jazz, you will sometimes hear sixteen-bar blues or even eighteen-bar blues with more chord substitutions. Experiment with playing different shuffles, jazz swing, 12/8, and funky grooves over the twelve-bar blues form. See more on the blues and shuffles in my book *Blues Drumming* (Hal Leonard).

 Track 4 features a Chicago-style shuffle over a twelve-bar blues form.

TRACK 4

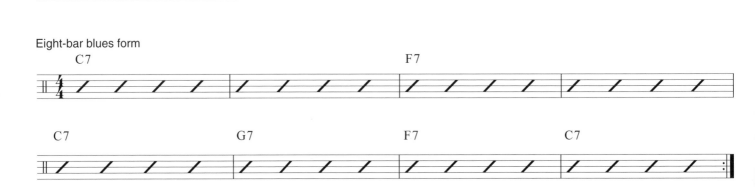

Twelve-bar blues form

Eight-bar blues form

Here are some additional grooves, fills, and phrases in the blues style with which to experiment.

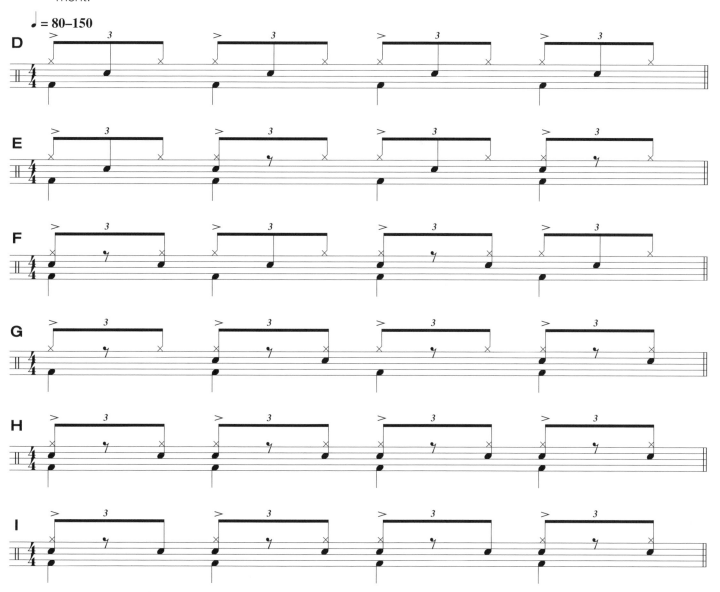

The following are two-beat fills coming from the groove.

The next examples feature fills and ensemble phrases.

M Fills and ensemble phrases

N

O

BUSINESS

After my first record date as a drummer when I was nineteen years old, I was excited to report to studio guitar legend Tommy Tedesco how great the rhythm section was, and what a good time I'd had. He looked at me and said, "Did you get paid? Did you get your money?" I said, "Yes," and Tommy replied, "That's all that matters." Of course, we both new other things mattered, but he was right on the money. I never forgot Tommy's advice of that day. If being a musician is your business, you must treat it as just that—a business.

The following are a few tips to get you thinking about and conducting the business side of drumming. Stay in touch with virtually all musicians, composers, and producers that you know and have worked for in the past: i.e., network. If you're just getting started, go to clubs and try to sit in to be heard. Have a good attitude. Do not bug people. There is a way to keep in touch with people without being a pain. Respect people's time and they'll respect and remember your awareness, even if they're busy at the moment. Other drummers need subs and will recommend you if they like the way you play and if you take care of business. The two most important things you can do are: 1) be on time, and 2) be prepared for the job.

Email is a great way to stay in touch with your contacts and let them know what you have been up to. All of your invoices, biographical info, credentials, and budgets can be sent via email. Use discretion, however, in sending unsolicited group emails, which can do more damage than good in an ever-growing world of cyber-junk. A good rule of thumb is either to share a piece of new information (such as info on your upcoming gig), or to genuinely thank someone for his/her kindness. Communications that simply ask for something can be unwelcome, considered an annoyance, and end up in the trash. Alternatively, when used wisely, email enables you to get things done quickly and efficiently. Another advantage is that you have a running documentation of what was said in a business exchange as well as when it took place. Since I've starting using email in my daily business routine, the line, "It must have been a misunderstanding" (a comment that had previously been the occasional product of an undocumented telephone conversation), no longer holds water. With email, "memory lapses" are easily cleared up with a click or two of the mouse. Of course, there is no substitute for a real-time conversation over the phone or a face-to-face meeting, but every business transaction made in those situations should be documented in a same-day follow-up email to ensure clarity and protection to all parties. For example, "It is my understanding from our meeting this morning that…." Everyone is busy. Mastering email to grow and protect your interests can serve as an invaluable asset.

If you are going on tour with an artist, here are a few things that you'll want to discuss with the management, label, or music director (MD): Be sure to get all agreements in writing before packing your bags. Create your own deal memo. The deal memo focuses on the important issues regarding what it is you need to do the job (i.e., make a list of the things you need). A more detailed contract can then be signed (if needed) after both parties have agreed on the major deal points. A list might include:

- Weekly salary amount
- Weekly per diem amount
- My own hotel room
- Round-trip plane ticket
- Drum tech
- Rehearsal schedule
- Weeks on tour

It's always good to run your business scenarios by a trusted attorney and/or accountant before making final decisions. Remember, if you take care of business first, you will be able to relax and focus on the job at hand, performing at your undistracted best.

Become a member and get involved in organizations tied into your industry, such as the following:

- Local musicians union (hint: always have scale sheets on hand)
- Percussive Arts Society (PAS)
- International Association of Jazz Educators (IAJE)
- National Academy of Recording Arts and Sciences (NARAS)

Stay focused—business first, then groove your heart out!

BOSSA NOVA

Bossa Nova is a style of Brazilian music that was made popular in the late 1950s in Rio de Janeiro's south side. It's in 4/4 time, and uses a cross stick rhythm on the snare drum based on the Latin clave rhythm (see *Clave* p. 27).

Forward clave for bossa

Reverse clave for bossa

The first bossa nova single was the Getz/Gilberto recording of "The Girl from Ipanema"; it was perhaps the most successful of all time. The genre would withstand substantial watering down by popular artists over the next four decades. The bossa nova has the same ostinato bass drum rhythm as the samba. The difference is that the bossa nova is in 4/4 time, and the samba is in 2/2, also known as cut time; see more under *Samba* (p. 107). In America, bossa novas are normally played more slowly than sambas. Traditionally, this is not always the case. Bossa novas can be up-tempo and sambas can be medium or slow tempos, though the opposite can be true as well.

TRACK 5

Listen to **Track 5** (Example A) and then learn the bossa nova grooves below. Saturate your-self in the style by listening to different bossa novas. This will help you develop your time-feel in the style.

A Forward clave

B Reverse clave

BO DIDDLEY BEAT

Bo Diddley (born December 30, 1928) is an American rock 'n' roll guitarist, singer, and songwriter whose pumping rhythm-guitar style became an often-imitated trademark in the progression of rock 'n' roll. Bo Diddley and his persistent, primitive, even violent guitar sound is often credited with strongly influencing the transition of blues into his signature outside-of-the-mainstream style of rock 'n' roll. He stood out for being on the fringe of 1950s rock 'n' roll, and is known for the "Bo Diddley beat," based on the rumba or clave rhythm (see example A below, and *Clave*, p. 27), which in turn grew out of roots in West Africa. The rhythm resembles "hambone," a style used by street-corner bands in which Bo Diddley and others patted the beats out on their person by slapping their legs, arms, chest, and cheeks while singing vocal phrases.

The Bo Diddley beat is a two-bar rhythmic phrase. The next example demonstrates this beat, showing the clave rhythm in the accents.

A

The rhythm has been a huge influence on many rock 'n' roll artists such as Buddy Holly ("Not Fade Away"), The Who ("Magic Bus"), Bruce Springsteen ("She's the One"), U2 ("Desire"), George Michael ("Faith"), and the Rolling Stones ("Not Fade Away").

Artists who have covered Bo Diddley songs include the Rolling Stones, The Animals, Bob Seger, The Who, The Yardbirds, The Doors, Eric Clapton, and Aerosmith. The half-time shuffle that Jeff Porcaro played on the Toto song "Rosanna" was a combination of the John Bonham (Led Zeppelin) groove on "Fool in the Rain," the Bernard Purdie groove on Steely Dan's "Babylon Sisters," and the Bo Diddley beat.

The next example features a four-bar eighth-note groove using the 12" and 14" toms over to a snare backbeat, with a half-note bass drum and hi-hat quarter-note pulse. The groove is slightly swung.

TRACK 6

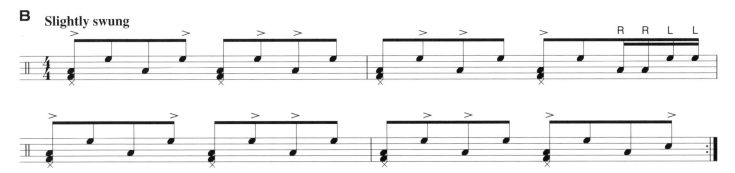

B **Slightly swung**

Write and experiment with some of your own grooves influenced by the Bo Diddley beat and time-feel. Don't forget to do some listening to the artists previously mentioned. The groove lives on in these and other similar songs.

BALLADS

In jazz and popular music, a *ballad* is a short song in a slow tempo, usually with a romantic or sentimental vibe in the lyric. The term is also used for purely instrumental pieces.

Playing ballads in a jazz or pop style is not easy for the drummer because the tempos can be very slow at times. I remember working with Jeff Porcaro on a record I was producing and arranging, and one of the songs was a classic Stevie Wonder tune. The tempo was around ♩ = 55 bpm. Jeff built that song beautifully from beginning to end using a lot of space and dynamics, and the tempo stayed right there. You are advised to check out some of the ballads on the Toto records to hear these great performances by Jeff Porcaro.

Jazz ballads are usually played with brushes on the drumset. The drummer stirs the soup with the brushes. See the diagram shown below.

TRACK 7

Track 7 consists of eight bars of a slow jazz ballad that was not recorded with a click, so it breathes and has a rubato feel. *Rubato* is defined as a dwelling on some notes and a hurrying of others. The CD track features drums playing with brushes and upright bass.

The following list highlights a few of my favorite jazz ballads. Look these up and give them a listen.

"Body and Soul," Harold Arlen (Coleman Hawkins version)

"My Funny Valentine," Rodgers and Hart (Miles Davis version)

"God Bless' the Child," Billie Holiday

"Naima," John Coltrane

"In a Sentimental Mood," Duke Ellington

"'Round Midnight," Thelonious Monk

RH
1, 2, 3, 4

LH
1, 2, 3, 4

Spend some time working on your pop and jazz ballad time-feels. Remember, there is a lot more space in between each note when you are playing a slow ballad. If you are in the studio and recording a slow ballad with a click track, always ask for an eighth-note click (subdivided pulse). It will be much easier for you to lock in and groove with the eighth-note click than with a quarter-note click. Then relax, take a breath, and play.

CLICK TRACKS

A "click track" acts as a metronome in the studio. When I play with a click track, I like the click sound to be a cowbell sample with a good attack, short decay, and a tone that fits into most tracks. I have a custom cowbell click that I track along to in my studio, and I take it with me to other studios on a firewire drive. This way I can pretend I'm playing with a percussionist who is laying down a quarter-note cowbell part.

For a good exercise, get yourself an egg shaker (cost: two dollars at any music store), and practice playing shaker parts to a click track, both with and without music. Listen back and make sure your part is with the click and that the shaker feels good. Once you are confident that you can make a shaker pass with any track at any tempo, try it the next time you are work-ing in a studio. Suggest to whoever you are working for that you want to make a shaker pass for yourself with which you can play along. This way you can play to your shaker pass with the track, and lower the volume of the click (cowbell) in your headphones. This enables you both to lock into your own time-feel and to avoid asking for more click. The shaker part is to be heard only by you in your cue mix. They don't need to hear it in the control-room playback mix. If they want to use your shaker part in any part of the song later, they will have it. Once you get a good headphone mix of the track (between the click and shaker), you can sit back, relax, and groove. If your time-feel and groove are down the middle of the time, you can cancel out the click. Remember that the click is only a guide and not intended to be part of the track. I always pretend that the click is following me and have found that much easier to accomplish when the sound is a cowbell.

Track 8 features a full band and includes a quarter-note cowbell click as opposed to other click sounds that you may hear, like weird bell tones, sampled side stick, or other electronic clicks.

TRACK 8

If you were tracking with a rhythm section (as opposed to overdubbing), without loops or other sequenced tracks in the song, and you happened to rush the click on the outro of the song and the band followed you, that can still be a usable take if the vibe and groove were happening, and everyone moved in time together. However, if you are in grid mode in Pro Tools and you are tracking to loops and/or sequenced tracks, you have to play down the middle of the time so everything lines up in the end when they are finished with all the cut-and-paste Pro Tools edits.

Also work on playing with different clicks at different tempos. **Track 9** features the same band as **Track 8**, but without drums. Play along and record yourself with **Track 9**, and listen back to

TRACK 9

see where you're putting the time-feel in relation to the cowbell click.

CYMBALS

A cymbal is a musical instrument consisting of a slightly concave round brass plate that is either struck against another cymbal or struck with a stick.

Choosing the right cymbals for a live or studio job can be tedious at times with so many different manufacturers and cymbals to choose from. When I'm working on a project, my cymbal selection is based on the style and vibe of the music. First, I choose the drumset and drumhead configu-ration that will be used. After the kit is set up and tuned, I start to think about the cymbals. If it's a rock vibe and it's

Paiste Traditional series cymbals

loud, and I want to bash yet still have the cymbals sound musical, I go with my Paiste Giant Beats 24" ride, 18" and 20" crashes, and 15" hi-hats. What I really like about these cymbals is that they are not really heavy, but you can rock on them and they are very musical (listen to **Track 58**, Punk). They are the re-issue of the cymbals that John Bonham used with Led Zeppelin in the beginning.

Remember to choose cymbals that complement the group or artist with whom you're working. If the singer is female and has a soft voice, you do not want to use heavy cymbals. The opposite is true if it is a male singer who really belts it out. Experiment with different rides, crashes, and hi-hats until you find which sound works nicely under the voice. For jazz or softer pop music, I like to use Paiste Traditionals. (Listen to **Track 7** to hear a ballad played with Traditionals.)

For louder pop/rock I go with Paiste Dark Energy or Signature rides, crashes, and hi-hats. Combinations vary depending on the music. (Listen to **Track 36** to hear the Dark Energy rides in a hard rock setting.)

For funk, hip-hop, or heavy metal, I like to mix and match different sets. I really like the Paiste Noise Works (listen to **Track 34**, Heavy Metal), as these specialty cymbals are great for creating new darker sounds. The old Paiste 2002 Sound Edge hi-hats are also great for rock (as demonstrated on **Track 66**).

The Paiste Alpha series has some great sensitive China cymbals that I've been using a lot. They're not so loud that they're overpowering, and they sound great whether you play them with mallets or with your hands (listen to **Track 54**). When you are selecting cymbals, think of yourself as an artist who is choosing the right pallet of colors for your musical canvas.

CARPET

When you're jobbing around town, doing rehearsals, clubs, shows, and casuals, you have to set up your drums on all kinds of surfaces. Sometimes there is not a carpeted surface on which to set up. You do not want your drumset to be moving around as you play. There is nothing worse than when your bass drum or hi-hat stand starts moving forward as you're trying to groove with the band. Make sure you have a good carpet with a rubber backing on it, rolled up and in your car at all times, and that it is large enough to accommodate your whole drumset. This way you don't have to worry about what kind of surface you'll be setting up on, and you can concentrate on groovin' rather than chasing after your drumset.

COMMUNICATION

The key to success in any relationship is communication. Whether you're conducting business, on the bandstand, or in the studio, keeping the lines of communication open is crucial to making a living as a drummer.

Keep your ears and eyes open. Let people talk, and really listen before you speak. You can learn a lot about a person or a situation by listening first and speaking once you have more information. When you do speak, it is most powerful to stick to the facts and keep it simple. Let the facts speak for themselves and avoid making judgments about others' intentions. Beware of going on and on and repeating yourself. Organize your thoughts and say what you need to say. Get in and get out.

With all the loops, samples and computer-driven sequenced tracks, everyone (producers, songwriters, engineers, musicians, and the cable guy) is a drum expert in today's music world. There will never be a shortage of people telling you what to play and what not to play.

Fielding a room full of experts requires patience and knowing what is working or not working within a piece of music. Always remember that you are in a given situation because you are the rhythm expert; so own it and act like it. Not that you should come from a place of inflated ego, but from a place of confidence in knowing your unique ability to bring to the table what is best for the music. You should always have three or four ideas that will work for the same situation. The good news is that with all the technology available today, people can play examples for you, demonstrating the direction in which they want to go. Listen, be open-minded, take direction without any attitude, and offer good ideas. Groove and play in service of the song and you will be fine.

When you're on the bandstand in a live situation, make sure your lines of communication are open. You want to be able to see the leader, conductor, or music director who is cueing you and the band. You should maintain frequent visual communication on stage. In addition to all this, remember to have fun, groove, and enjoy the ride. Music is not open-heart surgery. No one ever died from playing a bad note.

COMMON TIME

"Common Time" usually refers to 4/4 meter, which is often marked "**c**." Four beats to the measure (the quarter note gets the beat) is the time signature that drummers play in most of the time. But sometimes, because we are exploring odd meters or polyrhythms, we can forget how important common time is. Let's revisit 4/4 time for a minute. Spend time playing some of the grooves in your repertoire against both a whole-note and half-note bass drum phrase. This works great for rock, funk, hip-hop, and Latin grooves. Keep your hands and time-feel the same as always, but make the bass drum big and open, with no syncopation. This exercise will help you to feel the downbeat of beat 1 more strongly. It will also eventually make your time-feel wider within each bar when you return to playing the same grooves with the original syncopated bass drum rhythms. Also practice feeling the upbeats and down-beats of the sixteenth notes. This will help you to feel upbeats in time as strongly as you feel downbeats.

In the following examples, use A, B, or C as ostinatos in your bass drum, and play D, E, and F on your snare drum against the bass drum. Play each measure as a two-, four-, or eight-bar phrase.

Upbeat and Downbeat Rhythm Exercise

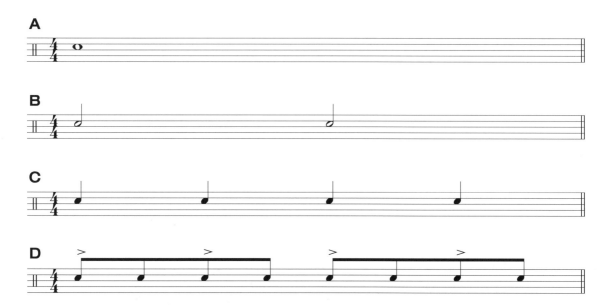

Most of the grooves that you play will have a feeling of downbeats, upbeats, or a combination of both. There's more on this subject under *Lope (of the Groove)* (p. 67) and *Rhythmic Guide* (p. 96).

CARE OF YOUR DRUMS

When you are running around town gigging, on the road traveling, or in the studio, attending to the care of your instruments is as important as your performance. If you are taking care of your instruments yourself and do not have the luxury of a drum tech, there are a few tips you can follow to make sure your equipment is well cared for.

Make sure you have the right equipment for the right job. Don't try to force one drumset on every musical situation in which you are involved. You don't want to take a rock kit to a jazz gig or vice versa. Try to have or build up to a couple of sets to choose from, and an assortment of snare drums and cymbals. This is your business and these are the tools of your trade. This will put less wear and tear on your equipment. Make sure your drumheads are in good shape so that you can tune your drums properly, which will enable you to sound your best. Keep your gear clean and free of dust. Treat your drums and cymbals like nice pieces of furniture. Your bass drum pedal and hi-hat stand should be well oiled to alleviate any squeaky sounds. Always have extra heads in your car, especially for the bass drum and snare drum. Also have an extra bass drum pedal and hi-hat stand. Throughout my career I've had brand-new pedals break on the first show. Weird things can happen at the worst times, so be prepared. Have snare string for your snare wires and a tool kit in your trap case. Protect your drums with cases. Padded soft cases are light and reliable for gigging around town. Hard cases are better for traveling on the road via plane, bus, etc. If you have lugs that are making noise, you will need to pack them, otherwise you will have problems when you record. Whether you or someone else is taking care of your equipment, it has to be done right or you will eventually sound wrong.

CONDUCTOR

The conductor is the leader or director of an orchestra, band, or chorus. He or she can be your most important ally.

I remember playing a show once in Vegas at the Thomas Mack Arena. I got a call in the middle of the night and was at the airport three hours later to replace a drummer who had been fired—not an ideal situation to go into. The show was three hours long with non-stop drumming. The band consisted of twenty-two horns and a seven-piece rhythm section. There were three shows on Saturday, and I was supposed to play all three without a rehearsal. The book was large and all the charts were either four or five pages long. Two things got me through that first day.

- **Number 1**: About a year earlier I'd seen Steve Gadd play with Chuck Mangione and his big band. I saw Gadd play the first night and the fifth night. I was told by someone backstage that Steve had not had a chance to rehearse with the band. The first night he sounded incredible, with great time and feel. I noticed he wasn't playing a lot of figures or fills, but just grooving hard, making the band feel right and setting up all the important parts of the songs and endings. On the fifth night, he sounded the same, but because he knew the book, he played a little more and added some great fills and ensemble setups. But his time-feel was the same as the first night—great grooves right in your face. What those two nights taught me were to make the band feel good at all costs and keep your place. Don't try to play everything on the page, especially if there is no time for a rehearsal.

- **Number 2**: Watch the conductor and make sure you have direct visual contact with him/her. Do not have your face so buried in the chart that you miss cues for tempo, meter, and dynamic changes. Since I had never played or heard the show, the conductor was my best ally. After I tuned my drums, I was going over some of the charts with the percussionist on the gig when the conductor arrived. As I introduced myself to him, he said to me, "Don't worry. Just watch me and I'll put this show right in your lap." And he did. As the first song was counted off, I remembered what Steve Gadd had done when I saw him a year earlier. I concentrated on three things: 1) groove hard and make the band feel good; 2) keep my place and nail transitions and endings; and 3) watch the conductor. After the first show ended, many of the horn players came up to me, hugged me, and said, "Thank you for making the band feel good."

Remember that if you don't play every written figure in the chart the first time, the world won't come to an end. Groove hard, make the band feel good, don't overplay, keep your place, and always watch the conductor. If you do these things, you too may get a hug.

CHARTS AND CHART NOTES

A chart is like a story. When you tell a story, you always enhance the most important parts while keeping pace within the story line. When you're reading a drum chart, lead sheet, or notes scribbled on a napkin, you need to sum up the story as quickly as possible so you know where you are going within the chart and song form.

The following two situations will help to illustrate the value of good chart reading. The first is when you have to learn a lot of songs in a short amount of time, and they just hand you a CD and some lead sheets or chord charts. Sum up the bars and sections of each song and make a chart that looks like the next example.

CHART NOTES • Song Name • Feel • Tempo

Intro: 8 bars

Verse 1: 16 bars

Chorus 1: 12 bars

Introlude*: 4 bars

Verse 2: 16 bars

Chorus 2: 12 bars

Bridge: 8 bars   ♩. ♪ ⅞ ♪ ⅞ ♪ ⅞ ♬ ‖ (Last bar of Bridge)

Solo: 12 bars

Chorus 3: 12 bars

Chorus

*__Introlude__: when the intro returns as an interlude within the body of the song.

These chart notes will go with the full chart that you have. They will enable you not to be buried in the sheet music, counting bars. It will help you to memorize the song form faster. Remember, you don't want to count when you are reading a chart. Only count when you have to. Always count tacet (silent) bars. Once you see and hear the rhythmic, harmonic, and melodic shape of a song, and can trust your ears, the process will get easier with experience. Write your chart notes out in pencil so it will be easy to make any changes. Your chart notes are just a condensed version of the song form. You can add key ensemble rhythm figures, unison lines, or endings—anything that is important for you to remember within the song form.

The second situation is when you are in a studio and you don't have a lot of time to check out the music before you start recording. Again, use the time that you do have wisely to create a chart note page from the chart that is in front of you. Commit to the grooves that you are going to play in each section of the song and trust your ears. Creating chart notes for any existing chart or from listening to a CD demo of the song will help you to be more organized and confident with the music at hand. Work on creating chart notes for yourself for all of your live and studio situations.

COUNTRY

Country is a musical style that originated among white populations in rural areas of the southern and western United States.

In 1949, the music industry adopted the name "country and western music" to replace the less politically correct term "hillbilly music." Its roots lie in the traditional folk music of Europeans who had settled in the Appalachians and other areas. With the advent of industrialization in the 1930s and '40s, white southerners migrated to urban areas, exposing them to the new influences of blues and gospel music. This included their themes of heartbreak that are so often identified with country music, which was widely accepted and embraced by the early 1970s.

Country produced two of the top-selling solo recording artists of all time. Billed as "The Hillbilly Cat," Elvis Presley was the first. He set into motion a clear path toward rock 'n' roll with his style of country music, sporting bluesy vocals and a strong back beat, which earned him the popular nickname of "The King." Garth Brooks is the other top-selling country music solo artist. Another giant was Johnny Cash, a multi GRAMMY® Award-winning and profoundly influential American country and rock 'n' roll singer and songwriter. Alongside Cash was his musical wife, country singer and songwriter June Carter Cash.

Country and rock are the most popular radio formats in America as of 2007, reaching 77.3 million adults weekly, which is virtually 40 percent of the adult population. Among contemporary country stars (1981–2007) are the Dixie Chicks, Clint Black, Garth Brooks, Faith Hill, Vince Gill, Reba McEntire, Carrie Underwood, and Shania Twain. Nashville drummers to listen to include Larrie Londin and Paul Leim.

The first example below (**Track 10**) features a groove called a "train beat," which is played on the snare drum with Blasticks. You can also use standard sticks or brushes with this beat. There is a slight swing feel in the groove. The second example is a classic country two-beat feel. Practice both grooves, then go back and do some listening to get the feel.

TRACK 10

A Train beat

B Classic country/two-beat

COMMIT

Committing to your instrument is a lifelong endeavor. As with any relationship, it takes much time and energy. Here are a few tips to consider:

- Commit to a practice schedule.

- Stay focused. Don't let people or things distract you when it's time to work on your craft.

- When you take a job, be 110% committed, or don't take it.

- Commit to the groove.

- If you're in a band, be committed and be on time to rehearsals and gigs. If it's not working for you anymore, get out.

- Be committed in all your work and personal relationships.

- Remember that being self-employed in the music business is about three things: relationships, relationships, and relationships.

- If you're studying music in school or with a private instructor, be committed to your classes and private lessons. Put the time in and do the work. This will pay off in a big way down the road.

- Treat people the way you want to be treated—with respect.

- When you can, help others (i.e., give back).

I'm sure you have a few of your own to add to this list. Think about it and commit to your drumming career.

COUNT-OFF

When you're onstage or in the studio and you are not using a click track, you will sometimes be responsible for counting in the band. How you go about doing this will greatly affect the way the band sounds on the first downbeat of the song. I can't tell you how many times in my career it has happened that someone else counted off a song and either the tempo was way off, or the count-off was barely audible. You do not want to fall into the category of the lazy count-off. Since you are not a computer, you should have a small digital click box with a flashing light so you can find the tempo if you have time in between songs. If you don't have time, you need to pull the tempo up from memory using your internal clock. Think of the melody and groove in your head, and that will help you to find the tempo that you have internalized for the song. If you are in 4/4 time, you may wish to do a two-bar count-off. Count the song off with authority while clicking your sticks. Click eight quarter notes for the two bars while you're counting in half time for the first bar, and quarter notes for the second bar.

Make sure everyone in the band can hear your count-off, and that you are counting with the vibe and energy of the song that you are going to play. Remember, the whole groove of the band is going to come from your count-off. Having the right time-feel for that first downbeat comes from your count-off. Think about it and make it count.

CHANGING METERS

As drummers, we should be able to flow and groove seamlessly from one time signature to the next. Listen to **Track 11** and follow the changing-meters chart below.

TRACK 11

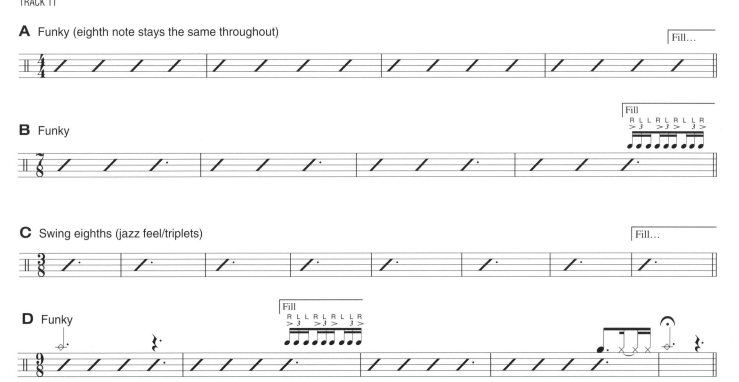

The above chart shows a funky eighth-note groove that is slightly swung in the 4/4, 7/8, and 9/8 sections. The 3/8 section is a jazz feel with swing eighths. The eighth note stays the same throughout the chart. The cowbell click is a quarter note or quarter note-dotted quarter combination, depending on the eighth-note subdivision. See the following notes for the form:

A	4/4 section	4 bars / funky / slightly swung
B	7/8 section	4 bars / funky / slightly swung
C	3/8 section	8 bars / swing eighths / jazz feel
D	9/8 section	4 bars / funky / slightly swung

In the next example, the basic grooves, fills, and ensemble figures for each section of the chart have been notated. Learn these and then have a go at **Track 12**, which includes the same click and shaker as **Track 11**, but without the drumset part. After you've played this

TRACK 12

example with the chart, make up some of your own grooves and fills to play with along with **Track 12** using the chart. Have fun and groove with changing meters.

A Funky, slightly swung

B Funky, slightly swung

C Swing 16ths, Jazz feel

D Funky, slightly swung

For more on this topic, see *Odd Meters* (p. 78), as well as in my book/CD *Drummer's Guide to Odd Meters* (Hal Leonard).

COWBELL

Drumset players should be able to play basic studio overdubs or live parts on some of the standard hand percussion instruments. Let's start with the cowbell (more cowbell!… just kidding). The standard rock cowbell part consists of four quarter notes. Practice playing a quarter-note cowbell to any rock or pop track. Work on getting a consistent sound and groove. On **Track 13**, the cowbell part is an African rhythm played against a shaker and two djun-djuns. This part is more syncopated than the 4/4 quarter-note rock cowbell part that you have been working on.

TRACK 13

African cowbell rhythm

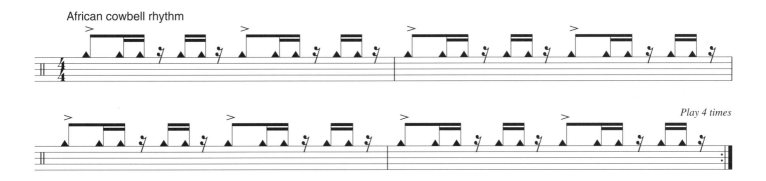

Practice playing this rhythm as an overdub, away from the drumset. Then, set up a cowbell on your drumset and use it for rhythms that you would normally play on your hi-hat or ride. This will incorporate a new sound into your kit. For more information on cowbell and bell parts, check out my books/CDs from the *World Beat Rhythms Series*: *Brazil*, *Africa*, and *Cuba* (Hal Leonard).

CLAVE

The clave rhythmic pattern is not to be confused with the percussion instrument known as the claves, a pair of cylindrical hardwood sticks. The pattern's roots are found in West African music, which paved the way for further development in Cuba as a rhythmic guide. The clave pattern serves as a rhythmic timeline for virtually all Afro-Cuban music (i.e., salsa). "Clave" translated from Spanish means "key," and consists of a rhythmic structure built around the melody of a song and its phrasing. The rhythmic phrases of the clave are recognized as a defining feature and structural element in Cuban music.

The clave may serve as a framework to which the whole musical arrangement must relate. Much of this depends upon the style being played and the musicians playing it. Whether the clave is forward (as in the following example) or reverse (i.e., switch the order of the two measures of the following example) is usually dictated by the phrasing of the melody.

The *son clave* is the most common type of clave rhythm in Cuban popular music.

Son clave

The above is said to be in the 3-2 direction because there are three notes in the first measure and two in the second. The pattern is the same for the 2-3 clave, but with the measures reversed.

The *rumba clave* is another type, often associated with a more folk-like style. As shown below, it too is found in both the 3-2 and the 2-3 directions, but the 3-2 is more common.

Rumba clave

Often called the *6/8 clave*, the third Cuban clave is a variation on the familiar West African 12/8 timeline. It is played mainly in older styles such as the rumba Colombia, and is a cowbell pattern.

6/8 son clave

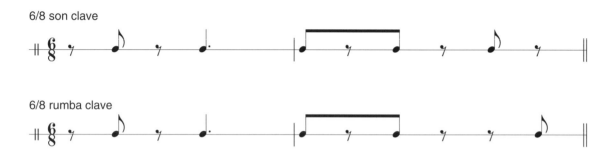

6/8 rumba clave

Practice the clave rhythms and incorporate them into your grooves in any style that you are playing. For more information on clave rhythms as applied to the drumset, check out the following book/CD packages: *Afro-Cuban Coordination for Drumset* and *In the Pocket: Grooves and Fills Based on Latin Clave Patterns*, both published by Hal Leonard Corporation.

DYNAMICS

The expression marks and the signs indicating the loudness and softness of tone are commonly referred to as the "dynamics" of a composition. Learning to play at different dynamic levels will take much time and patience. The following list includes some of the most common dynamic markings (symbols)—memorize them. Music directors, composers, producers, and other musicians will constantly tell you to play at certain volume levels ranging from soft to bashing loud. Sometimes you will have to make these dynamic adjustments in a few short bars of music. Practice, think about it, and get used to it.

Pianissimo: very soft (*pp*)

Piano: soft (*p*)

Mezzo: medium, half (*m*)

Mezzo piano: medium soft (*mp*)

Mezzo forte: medium loud (*mf*)

Forte-piano: attack strong, then soft at once (*fp*)

Forte: loud, strong (*f*)

Fortissimo: very loud (*ff*)

Crescendo: swelling, increasing the volume gradually (⟍)

Decrescendo/Diminuendo: decreasing the volume gradually (⟍)

Using dynamics when you're playing will help you to build tension and release within the music. Practice playing your grooves, fills, ensemble figures, and solos at different dynamic levels, and in all styles that you play. Work on building a groove from soft to loud while keeping the feel and vibe the same.

TRACK 14

Track 14 is a funky march groove that builds up from piano (*p*) to forte (*f*), from beginning to end. After listening, try some dynamic grooves of your own. Remember, using dynamics gives you somewhere to go within the piece. If everything is always loud, you can never take the listener on a dynamic journey. Playing dynamics helps to draw the listener into the music.

DRUM AND BASS CONNECTION

Locking in with the bass player is essential when you, as the drummer, are trying to create a forward-moving time-feel in the groove. The drummer and bass player should work together to create a basic foundation that grooves and inspires the rest of the rhythm section to add their parts and play with you. In all styles of music, your relationship with the bass player is a huge responsibility. Trying to get the drummer to lay back the groove or play down the middle of the time when the bass player is playing on top of the beat can be maddening. Both drummers and bass players need to make time-feel adjustments within the style to accommodate the right feel for the song being played. Having the ability to listen to each other and find parts that work together is a must.

The next example is a drum and bass groove featuring a reggae/rock feel, similar to a Stewart Copeland (Police) groove. Listen to the quarter-note bass drum pulse and notice how the syncopated hi-hat and bass play off each other. The hand drum (klong-yaw) and tambourine complement and add color to the groove. The example below shows only the first four bars of **Track 15**. Listen to the track and it will get you started hearing and seeing the rhythmic and melodic relationships between the drums and the bass.

TRACK 15

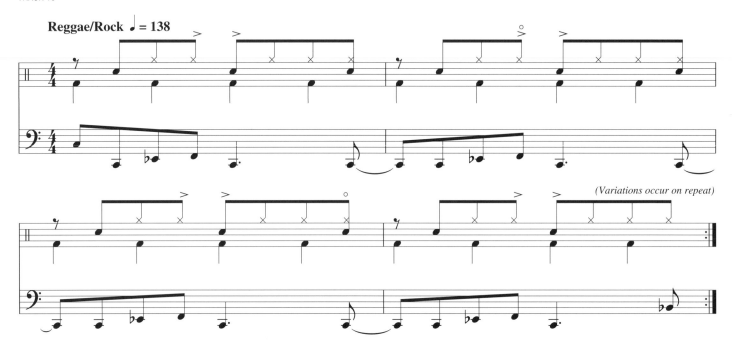

Throughout the history of music, there have been many great drum and bass connections. A few of these legendary pairings are listed below.

> Paul McCartney and Ringo Starr (The Beatles)
>
> John Paul Jones and John Bonham (Led Zeppelin)
>
> John Entwistle and Keith Moon (The Who)
>
> Leland Sklar and Russ Kunkel (Jackson Browne)
>
> David Hungate, Mike Porcaro, and Jeff Porcaro (Toto)
>
> Flea and Chad Smith (Red Hot Chili Peppers)
>
> Sting and Stewart Copeland (Police)
>
> Noel Redding and Mitch Mitchell (Jimi Hendrix Experience)
>
> Eddie Gomez and Steve Gadd (Chick Corea)
>
> Jimmy Garrison and Elvin Jones (John Coltrane)
>
> Jeff Porcaro and Abe Laboriel, Sr. (L.A. sessions)

Remember to begin by going back in time to explore great pairings of the past, then move onward to the present. For more information on the drum and bass connection, please check out my book *Rock Drumming Workbook* (Hal Leonard).

DRUM MACHINE

A drum machine is an electronic musical instrument designed to sequence drum and percussion samples into programmed grooves that can be plugged into songs. It can also be used as a practice tool to set up click tracks and drum and percussion beds to which one can play along.

I remember being in the studio in 1985 with Joe Sample. Looking around the room, I noticed Joe was sitting at a MIDI grand piano in the control room and the rest of us were surrounded by boxes, drum machines, synth modules, and samplers. I joked that if we didn't know each other we wouldn't know what instruments the other people played. I spent a lot of time during the '80s programming drum machines and doing drum overdubs over programmed grooves. During that era, the way we worked changed forever. It was all about the new sound of the day, and I jumped on the bandwagon and got into it. I've always looked at drum machines, samplers, sequencers, computer sequencing (Pro Tools), and loops as extensions of what you already do as a rhythmatist. Because I was a composer and music producer during that time as well as a drummer, I think it was easier for me to accept the change. I don't care what anyone says, there is nothing better than real drums moving air with a great drummer behind the wheel. But I also have a ton of programmed beats and loops in my library, and every groove has its place when it's in the right piece of music.

Some History

Released in 1980, the Linn LM-1 Drum Computer was the first drum machine to use digital samples. Interestingly, there were only 500 manufactured, but its distinct sound helped to launch the drum-machine revolution. It was so distinct that it set the tone for pop music in the following decade. The Linn LM-1 can be heard on Gary Numan's "Dance" and Prince's "1999" and "Purple Rain."

An attractive feature of the LM-1 was that each voice was tunable as a separate entity with individual outputs. Often two chips were triggered at the same time to compose many of the drum sounds the LM-1 could produce. In 1982, a more affordable version with fewer tunable voices, known as the LM-2 (a.k.a. the Linn Drum), was released. As the 1980s progressed, the Linn Drum fast became the industry standard for pop music production. Like the LM-1, this cheaper rendition featured sound chips that could be swapped out, as well as a crash sound that was included as standard.

Some well-known recordings that featured the Linn Drum include Michael Jackson's "Billie Jean" and "Thriller," The Cars' "Heartbeat City," Toto's "Africa," and Men Without Hats' "Rhythm of Youth." In 1983, synthesized music came into its own with the release of Yamaha's DX-7 and MIDI (musical instrument digital interface). MIDI involved transmitting musical data between digital components, such as between a computer's sound card and a synthesizer, which were then stored as waveforms on a chip to produce a specific sound.

A fertile year for drum machines, 1980 also gave rise to the Roland TR-808. Though it was not equipped with digital samples, its sound had a decidedly unique character, and drum machines using digitally sampled sounds were becoming more desirable. In 1983, the TR-909 was released, and in a short while it and its predecessor, the TR-808, would become a staple of the dance club, hip-hop, and techno styles. This was due in great part to its affordability as compared to the Linn Drum, as well as its appealing, analog-generated sound. It wasn't until the latter part of the 1980s that the TR-808's sound gained popularity (this was, ironically, approximately five years after the model had been discontinued). Beats of both the Roland TR-808 and TR-909 can be heard in a wide variety of rap, hip-hop, and pop music from the 1980s through present day. Eventually, the AKAI MPC-60 was manufactured. It was soon broadly used by rap and hip-hop artists, acting as a sequencer and drum machine all in one. We still hear the MPC-60 on many recordings in these styles.

Today

Nowadays, many musicians (myself included) work on a Mac-based (DAW) system like Pro Tools. On these systems, drum machines and samplers are digital plug-ins (software) that work as extensions of, or within, your main music production program. See more on this subject in *Pro Tools* (p. 87) and *Studio Tips* (p. 105).

DANCE (FIND YOUR DANCE)

I'm a terrible dancer. My partner, Claudia, is a very good dancer. At social functions she occasionally asks me to dance with her. This procedure usually ends with me trying to follow her on the dance floor. I let her lead and she can only do one thing, which is to make me look good, because I'm so bad.

Finding your dance behind the drumset should be fairly natural. The next time you're out listening to live music or watching a music DVD, spend some time watching how the drummer is moving behind the drums to the music he/she is playing. That movement is the drummer's dance for that groove or time-feel. For example, because samba is "in two," your body needs to move in two to feel two. Just watch Alex Acuña play a samba; you'll see that his body is dancing in two.

You should not be concerned or self-conscious of how you think you look, or be concerned with what other people might think. To get more comfortable with this, try just moving to the music. First try this when you are away from the drumset, and after that, pick up a shaker. Play the shaker and then get behind the kit and start playing. Feel the groove, let go, and find your dance within the groove. This natural movement is your own dance, and it should help you to relax into the groove.

DISCO

Disco is a genre of dance-oriented pop music that blends elements of funk and soul music with a strong quarter-note bass drum pulse. Disco was born in the dance clubs (discos) of cosmopolitan cities such as New York, in the 1970s. One attraction of disco was how it was presented in these venues—there were no musicians onstage, making the dancers the stars. By the mid-'70s, the disco groove and style was at the top of the mainstream pop charts. Most disco songs had large vocal ranges that dance around a steady "four-on-the-floor" bass drum beat, with an eighth-note or sixteenth-note hi-hat phrase, and an open hi-hat on the off-beat lope of the groove. Syncopated or dominating eighth-note octave bass lines are present at the bottom end of the groove. A quarter note at 120 bpm was the main tempo for disco hits.

I remember catching the tail end of the era when I arrived in Los Angeles in 1978. The recording sessions were always a groove with five- or six-piece rhythm sections and horns. Man, it really forced you to get your four-on-the-floor time-feel together with the click track. I remember hanging out at sessions with drummers Ed Greene and James Gadson. Those two guys really had that feel down. I learned a lot from hanging out with them at those sessions, and was able to put the knowledge to good use on my own sessions at the time.

Disco performers of particular note and chart-topping success included the Bee Gees, Donna Summer, the Village People, the Jackson 5, ABBA, Barry White, and Rod Stewart. Even a number of previously established artists recorded disco songs when it was at its pop-culture peak. Films such as *Thank God It's Friday* and *Saturday Night Fever* helped to fuel disco's rise in mainstream popularity. Although disco music's wide appeal declined in the early 1980s, it had an undeniable influence on the development of the house and techno music genres of the 1980s and early 1990s. It also played a role in the development of R&B and funk artists in the post-disco era.

The next examples feature three disco grooves. **Track 16** plays Example A a couple times, then varies the pattern a bit. Practice them and then write some grooves of your own in the disco vein. Don't forget to go back in time and do some listening.

TRACK 16

ENERGY

Being a drummer requires great output of energy when you are performing live and in the studio. Your body and mind need to be on the same page to be consistent in all your performing endeavors. When you are on the road night after night, keeping your body fueled with the essentials is sometimes challenging. The following are a few basic habits to develop that will serve you well:

- Drink a lot of water.

- Try to eat fresh foods rather than fast food.

- Take vitamins.

- Get some cardio exercise: run, swim, or use a treadmill at the hotel, if available.

- Stretch, do some yoga, as well as sit-ups and push-ups, which are good for keeping your upper body strong and powerful.

- Don't burn yourself out by staying up late every night. Get proper sleep.

Come up with a routine that works for you and be consistent. Not that you can't have a good time, but stay focused on what your job is—to perform at your highest level. To accomplish this on a regular basis you have to stay focused. If you already have a workout routine that you're doing at home or at the gym, find ways to adapt so that you can continue it on the road. If you practice even a moderate degree of self-discipline, you'll find that your energy and endurance levels will be greater when it's time to groove.

EXERCISE

When I was a young adult, I went through periods of my career without exercising or doing yoga. Over the years, I have found that running, yoga, and meditation have helped my overall energy level. They have kept my head clear and my thoughts focused on the matter at hand. In today's music industry climate and in the future, you will spend almost half of your time conducting business in order to do what you do. Staying in shape will help you deal with the day-to-day grind of it. Lower back pain from sitting behind the kit, sore hands and arms, and tendonitis are a few problems you might encounter over the years. I once hurt the fulcrum of my right hand by lifting a couch (don't move furniture!). It took months for it to feel normal again. The following are a few tips that have helped me over the years:

Exercise Schedule: Get on a regular exercise routine. Cardio is a great support for drumming. Breathing is part of your groove. Join a gym, jog outside at a local track, or do whatever you will do, on a regular basis. The key to cardio health is consistency.

Stretching: Stay flexible so you don't injure yourself while playing the drums. Stretching is great to alleviate and prevent lower back pain. Open your hand wide, and close your fingers into a fist, then open them all the way again. Do this in time, to a pulse. This is a great stretching and strengthening exercise for your hands and fingers that can be done almost anywhere. Get on a program, attend a class, and learn to stretch correctly.

Yoga: Yoga is a self-tuning of the body, mind, and breath. After you've studied for a while and attended classes, you can do it alone anywhere. Once I started doing yoga regularly, the lower back pain I had developed from sitting behind the drumset for long periods of time was gone. My breathing was much better when I played. It will enable you to relax during stressful situations. Chances are you will also sleep better. Attend a yoga class!

Meditation: Take ten minutes each day to clear your head and meditate. Think positive thoughts in general, and especially before a show. See the performance happen in your mind and focus on everyone groovin' and having a good time, including the audience. This will help you to get centered for your performance. It's another way of warming up before a show.

Open-mindedness: Read books and open your mind to new ideas. This will exercise your mental flexibility as well, which in turn helps you maintain your sense of play.

EXPERIENCE

A basic precept of gaining knowledge that accumulates and matures into experience is that one must listen in order to learn. The following example illustrates one of the countless ways in which an aspiring drummer, early in his/her career, chooses to develop the essential skill of listening… or not. Paying mindful attention to how well you listen will not only serve you as a musician but as a person being with other people in a way that will determine whether your experience transforms into a career.

It is a universal truth that when one is talking, one cannot listen. For instance, when I was coming up as a young drummer, I would often hear drummers spend a lot of time talking about other drummers. For example, "I saw so-and-so play with so-and-so last night, and I could have played that gig just as well, if not better." First off, the person talking did not get the gig. It was the drummer on the gig who was getting the experience while the talker sat in the audience, talking.

Something can be learned from every performance if one's ears are open—even a sub-par performance. In addition, to state the obvious, talking negatively about a fellow musician serves no useful purpose. One can be the best player in the practice room, but in the real world, employment comes to those who get along with people (especially if the gig involves a long tour), and to those whose focus is on actually playing.

Within the first four bars of your playing, anyone with good ears can tell if you really know how to play. Then it's a matter of your overall groove, musicianship, reading ability, how you relate to the rest of the band, and the politics of business that determine if you're the right person for the gig. Be supportive of other players. Help someone if you can. Give back. If you are persistent, a good player, and exercise patience, you will slowly gain the experience and confidence you need to feel relaxed about who you are and what you have to say as a player. If people like the way you play and like you as a person, they will recommend you for work, and you will gain more experience. So let your playing do the talking. It's usually the best form of communication. The bottom line is, listen and learn. If you do this in earnest, the experience will follow.

ELECTRONIC DRUMS

Electronic drums produce sound with an electronic waveform generator or sampler rather than an acoustic vibration. In the '80s, electronic drumsets came on the scene, pioneered by Simmons. Terry Bozzio was using an electronic kit at the time with Missing Persons. I remember using my Simmons SDS-5 kit on tons of sessions for Gary Wright, Joe Sample, the Crusaders, jingles, and TV and film sessions. The combination of Simmons and real drums was huge during this time period. I would get calls to overdub tom fills to tracks or play a full hybrid kit. Then came the Roland Octapad. This was a pad to MIDI converter, with no sampled sounds onboard. You could trigger any sound source (drum machine, sampler, or synth) and assign it to eight different touch-sensitive pads with dynamic adjustments. The Drum Kat (Kat) was the other pad-to-MIDI converter that was very popular during the '90s. The Ddrum, the Roland D-20 electronic drumset, and the Roland Handsonic are popular today.

TRACK 17

Track 17 features the Drum Kat pad controller triggering samples in an EX-24 sampler in Logic (recording software).

Listed below are some of the companies that produce(d) electronic drum modules, trigger pads, and acoustic triggers:

- Dauz
- Ddrum
- Roland
- Sherpa
- Simmons (went out of business in 1993)
- Smarttrigger
- Staff Drum
- Yamaha

The majority of currently available standard electronic drum modules include trigger inputs for at least two cymbals, a kick, a minimum of three toms, a dual-zone snare (head and rim), and a hi-hat. Certain modules offer a foot controller that elicits open and closed sounds on the hi-hat or variations thereof. Many different sounds can be assigned to the drum pad of your choice. This gives the drummer a multitude of possible drumset sounds, including a rock, jazz, or ballad set. It is even used in place of acoustic drums when appropriate. This is often how the genre of industrial music is produced—using sampled sounds that are non-percussive. When in the studio or playing a live gig, total sound separation can be achieved by using the module's selector switch to configure a wide variety of drumset sounds.

EARS

As musicians, our ears are our most valuable asset. Thus, we must treat them with care. My own personal setback convinced me once and for all just how important this is.

At one point in my career I developed acoustic trauma in one ear. The nerve endings in my inner left ear were traumatized by excessive volume. I know how it happened: bass amps behind my head at loud volumes, with me playing loud backbeats with no earplugs, proved a recipe for inner-ear disaster. After seeing an ear, nose, and throat doctor, I was told that the pain and ringing in my ear would probably go away if I started protecting my ears when playing or listening to music at loud volumes. I was lucky. After making some changes and using earplugs, I was very fortunate not to have lost any hearing. My ear trauma eventually healed. I learned my lesson, and to this day, I take very good care of my ears.

Protect your ears! You can't have good ears if you lose your hearing. Playing at loud volumes over a period of time will affect your hearing if you don't wear protection. Do not let other musicians put amps directly behind your drumset and blast your head off. Be aware of the volume that is being generated around and behind your kit. Speak up and always have control of the monitor mix behind you so that you can relax and play. In the studio, do not have loud clicks in your headphones, ripping your head off and damaging your ears. When you are practicing at loud volumes, wear your earplugs. Hopefully you will not be playing at extremely loud volumes at all times, but if you are, you should seriously consider wearing earplugs. You only have one set of ears. Once you lose your hearing or part of your high, mid, or low range, you won't get it back.

Find earplugs that are comfortable and yet still allow the music through when you're playing. Have a pair custom made if you can't find over-the-counter plugs that work for you. Remember, you have to be able to hear to develop great ears.

ENSEMBLE FIGURES

Ensemble figures are rhythmic figures or phrases played by some or all of the band, which we as drummers often need to punctuate and orchestrate.

Also called *section figures*, these licks may consist of an accented note or group of notes played by a section of the ensemble or the ensemble as a whole. These background figures are usually played behind soloists and singers, and are written as cues above the staff.

The drummer must play these rhythms without disturbing the phrasing of the ride cymbal or hi-hat.

The move from a groove into an ensemble figure punctuation or setup should always come from the time-feel of the groove. It's important to be able to play the punctuated rhythm first, within the groove, before trying to set up the figure with a fill.

Track 18 features a Steve Gadd-style hands-together jazz shuffle in three eight-bar phrases, with a final phrase of six bars. The following chart maps out the different eight-bar phrases of the ensemble figures and the six-bar phrase ending on the CD.

TRACK 18

Ending phrase (six bars)

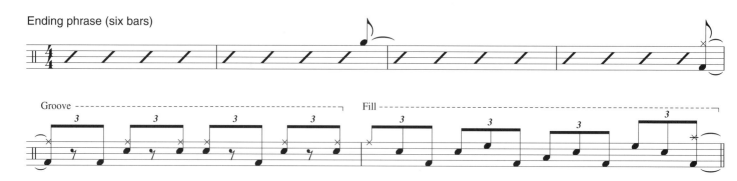

Important Ensemble Markings

(–) Legato: smooth and connected

(·) Staccato: separated; in a crisp, detached style

(>) Accent: indication to emphasize a note

(^) Short loud accent: indication to emphasize a note, but keep it short

(⌒) Fermata: indicates to hold a note (time stops)

After you listen to the CD, work on playing the jazz shuffle beat, and practice going into the ensemble figures. Play different fills of your own to set up the figures. Then practice the additional ensemble figures using the following procedure:

Play two, four, or six bars of any time-feel in any style, and then play the two-bar figure. Loop four-, six-, or eight-bar phrases together. Work on different styles, tempos, and dynamics.

A Additional ensemble figures

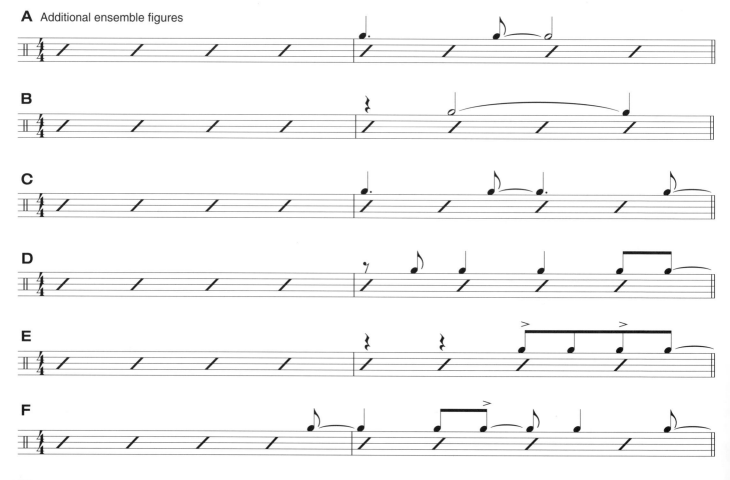

Remember that when you are sight-reading a chart, the most important thing is to groove and make the band feel good. If you miss a figure with the horns, life will go on, and you'll catch it next time.

FOCUS AND FINISH

If being a professional drummer is your goal, then you must stay focused. Don't let people or distractions keep you from being focused. You also need to finish what you start so you can move on to new things. I live by two words—*focus* and *finish*—to get all my projects, business, and personal endeavors done on time. Being focused helps you to finish. Finishing what you told yourself or someone else you would do is everything. Let's say I have a deadline to finish custom drum loops for a client, and on the day of the deadline I tell him/her that I'm not finished mixing the loops, but I'm 95% done. To the client who needs those loops, I might as well be half-way done. If I have a song that is 98% finished, but it's still on my hard drive, business-wise it's like having nothing, because it's unfinished and I can't work the song. If you have to learn thirty songs in five days for a gig, get on a schedule, map it out, stay focused, and finish. In your life you will have real deadlines and self-imposed deadlines—they are the same thing. You must get in the habit of focusing, finishing, and meeting all deadlines. Only then will people take you seriously in your profession as a drummer. The importance of this cannot be stressed enough. Stay focused and finish!

FUNK

The word "funk" originated from a slang term for "stink." Funk was the rawest form of R&B music. It was less structured than R&B, and the song forms expanded into extended jam sessions of Africanized rhythms built on subdivided and syncopated grooves. Funk originally appealed only to the hardcore R&B audiences. The most important aspect of funk music is the groove. The band moves and plays off of one another to create a time-feel that is of one entity.

Funk music uses low-end ostinato bass lines, keyboards, two rhythm guitar players playing single lines and riffs together, and a drum groove with a deep, syncopated pocket. Funk allowed for more freedom and improvisation within the song form than R&B. It was similar to what was going on around the same time in blues-rock, psychedelic, and hard rock.

Jimi Hendrix was a huge inspiration for funk guitar soloists. In the soul hits "Papa's Got a Brand New Bag" (1965) and "Cold Sweat" (1967) by James Brown, you can hear the roots of funk rhythms emerge. Sly and the Family Stone was influenced by soul, psychedelic, and rock, leaning into funk with the 1969 hit "Stand." But the official funk anthem was James Brown's 1970 "Get Up (I Feel Like Being A) Sex Machine."

George Clinton's Parliament and Funkadelic Ensemble turned funk into the ultimate party music with musicians, singers, and dancers onstage doing long, extended jams. When disco came into the picture in the mid-'70s, funk became smoother and lost some of its original earthiness. Funk also had a major influence on jazz (listen to Miles Davis's "The Man with a Horn" and "Tuttu"). In addition, it has also become a primary musical influence on hip-hop. Funk enjoyed a resurgence in the '90s among white audiences who wanted to explore the original classics.

Artists to listen to include Isaac Hayes; George Clinton; Prince; Michael Jackson; the Ohio Players; the Jacksons; Tower of Power; Chaka Khan; Average White Band; Rufus; the Isley Brothers; Herbie Hancock; Curtis Mayfield; Miles Davis; Stevie Wonder; Brecker Brothers; The Brothers Johnson; The Time; James Brown; Chic; Earth, Wind & Fire; Rick James; and Sly and the Family Stone.

These artists feature a wealth of outstanding funk drummers. Look for these drummers in other bands as well, and spend some time listening to their work.

Track 19 features a funk groove rhythmically similar to the James Brown hit "Cold Sweat" (1967), with Clyde Stubblefield on drums. The main groove for this track is represented in Example A below. It's very funky and syncopated. Also, check out the additional examples and work on these grooves for the time-feel.

TRACK 19

The next example shows what a chart might look like for the tune on **Track 19**. Notice the four-bar rhythmic turnaround at the end of the song form. This rhythm is heard in the clavinet part. In the third bar, the clavinet plays sixteenth notes subdivided into groups of twos and threes. The twos and threes make up four groupings of fives that go over the bar line and resolve on beat 2 of the fourth bar. Practice playing this rhythm on the snare drum against a quarter-note bass drum. You can then play around the clavinet part as on the CD, or play more with it. Experiment with this four-bar phrase coming from the time-feel of the groove. For more on this subject, check out my book/CD *Funk & Hip-Hop Drumming* (Hal Leonard).

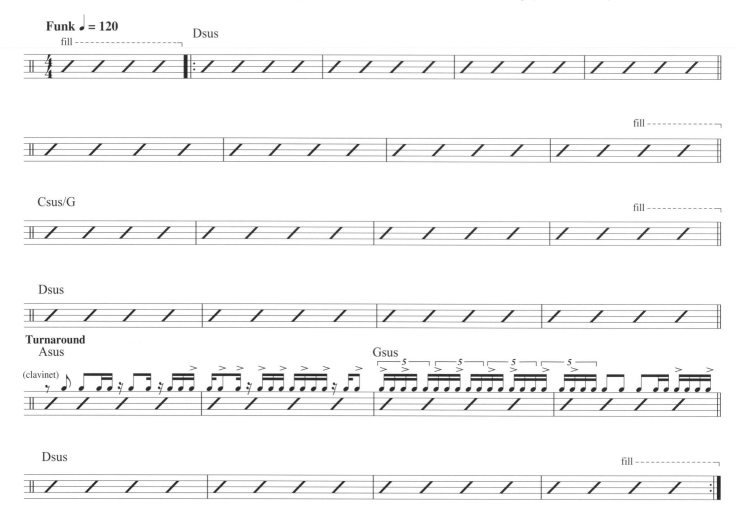

FIVE STEPS TO MUSICALITY

My *Five Steps to Musicality* are: 1) technique; 2) time; 3) time-feel; 4) phrasing; and 5) song form.

This is the second of two unique concepts that work together. The first concept is featured in *Rhythmic Guide Concept* (p. 96). Read this tip first, and then come back here to *Five Steps*.

Technique, time, time-feel, phrasing, and song form: the repetition of these steps using any rhythmic phrase is the key. If utilized properly, this concept will enable you to play any rhythmic phrase in any meter or style that you choose. By the end of Step 5, any rhythm you have chosen will be part of your musical vocabulary for life. Start off slowly. Do not go on to the next step until you have mastered the current step.

Let's run one of the rhythms from the *Rhythmic Guide Concept* down the *Five Steps*. In Steps 1 and 2, you are practicing your rhythmic idea. In Steps 3, 4, and 5, you are playing music with your rhythmic idea.

Step 1: Technique

    A. Count your idea groove out loud.

    B. Learn the sticking.

    C. Memorize the phrase.

Step 2: Time

    A. Play the idea groove on the snare drum using a metronome (as demonstrated on **Track 20**).

    B. Play the idea groove on the snare drum using your internal clock (**Track 21**).

Step 3: Time-feel

    A. Select a style (blues, shuffle, funk, samba, jazz, hip-hop, etc.).

    B. Play a basic groove in that style and sing a bass line or guitar riff against your idea groove. In this case, we'll use funk as an example. For more on the relationship between drumset and bass, see *Drum and Bass Connection* (p. 29).

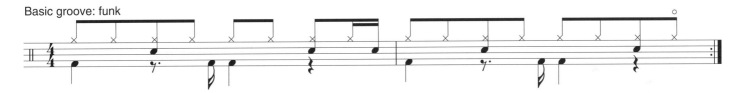

    C. Orchestrate your idea groove as a timekeeping phrase in that style.

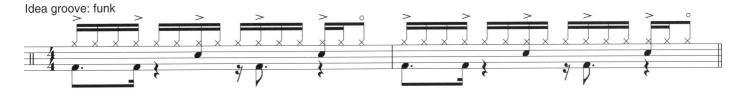

    D. Play two bars of the basic groove, then two bars of the idea groove. Repeat these four bars several times. Concentrate on making your idea groove come from the time-feel of your basic groove. Remember that you're developing your time-feel in the chosen style (note: do not use your idea groove as a fill yet).

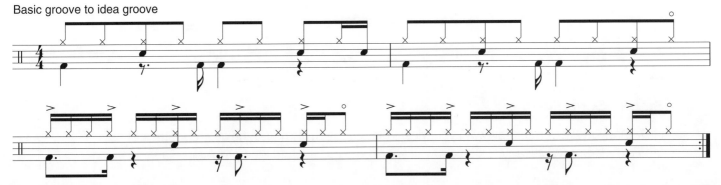

Step 4: Phrasing

A. Play different phrasing combinations:

- Two bars basic groove into two bars idea groove.
- Four bars basic groove into two bars idea groove.
- Four bars basic groove into four bars idea groove.
- Six bars basic groove into two bars idea groove.
- Eight bars basic groove into four bars idea groove.
- Eight bars basic groove into eight bars idea groove.

B. Think about different orchestrations, fills, ensemble figures, and dynamics. Make sure you work on different tempos. Sing ostinato (repetitive) bass lines out loud against your basic groove and idea groove while you're playing.

C. Phrasing Examples: Practice looping the following phrases, one into the next:

- Four bars of basic groove into two bars of idea groove.
- Four bars of basic groove into two bars of idea groove/fill.
- Four bars of basic groove into two bars of idea groove/ensemble figure.

TRACK 23

Step 5: Song Form

Now that you are comfortable with your new idea groove rhythm and the first four steps of the *Five Steps to Musicality*, it's time to put your basic groove and idea groove into a song form. These two grooves will make up phrases that relate to a song form. Mix up the phrasing and try different combinations of basic groove to idea groove, or idea groove/fill or idea groove/ensemble figure.

The next example is a twelve-bar blues form. Remember to practice singing a bass line while you're playing. After you can play and sing bass, practice singing a melody while you are playing. This will help you always to know your place in the song form, and to interact musically with the melody instrument, soloist, or vocalist in the ensemble. It will also help to keep you from stepping on the melody while you're playing. Groove, vocalize, and loop the song form.

TRACK 24

Twelve-bar blues form

Once you have mastered all the rhythms from the *Rhythmic Guides*, use the *Five Steps*, and experiment with different styles, meters, and rhythms. This should keep you busy for quite a while. You can learn more about these two concepts in my book/CD *Drummer's Guide to Odd Meters* (Hal Leonard).

FILLS

Fills are rhythms created for the purpose of occupying time. Once the groove has been established in a certain style, the drummer has to be able to flow from a groove into a fill and keep the time and time-feel steady. The feel of the fill should always come from the time-feel of the groove.

In Example A, the first two fills come from a straight-eighth slow rock groove in this six-bar phrase: two bars of the groove and a one-bar fill, then two bars of groove and a one-bar fill. The second fill is the same as the first, except it is double-time (twice as fast).

A Straight-eighth rock

The next group of fills comes from a hybrid groove that was influenced by the rhythms of the group Olodum from Northeast Brazil. Example B is twelve bars long: three and half bars of groove, followed by a half-bar fill within each four-bar phrase.

TRACK 26

B Olodum groove

Example C contains a group of fills played over a samba groove. The samba is "in two," and is often written in cut time (2/2). This example consists of a thirty-two-bar phrase: four bars of groove and four bars of fill, in alternation. This eight-bar cycle happens four times.

TRACK 27

C Samba

The next group of fills comes from a slow 6/8 funky blues feel. Example D is twelve bars long: three bars of groove and one bar of fill within each four-bar phrase.

D Fills

The last group of fills comes from a "four-on-the-floor" R&B groove that is slightly swung, with the hi-hat accented on the upbeats. Example E is twelve bars long: three or three and a half bars of groove and a one-bar or half-bar fill within each four-bar phrase.

E R&B fill (slightly swung)

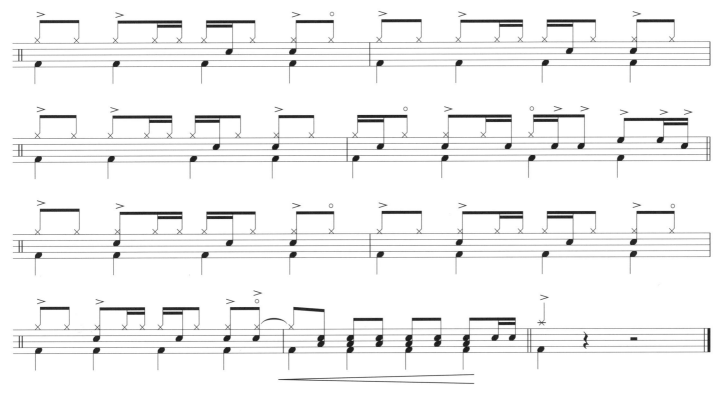

The following are some additional fill ideas that you can work on using different grooves up front. When you are done learning these fills, write some of your own and practice them within different styles.

F Additional fill ideas

GRIP

There are many ways to hold a drumstick. The grip you decide to use should be right for you. My grip changes depending on what style of music I'm playing. For example, if I'm playing jazz, softer funk grooves, or rudimental stuff on the snare drum, I will usually play using a *traditional grip*. If I'm playing harder and louder (rock, etc.), I will usually use *matched grip*. Sometimes I switch between the two grips in the same song. Matched grip is probably easier to learn because both hands use the same technique.

Matched grip

With matched grip, the stick will pivot between your thumb and the first joint of your index finger (this is your fulcrum). The fulcrum is where you hold and control the stick. The other fingers wrap around the stick loosely. Do not squeeze too hard as this can cause tension, which should be avoided at all costs. Relax and groove.

Traditional grip

With a traditional grip, the right hand (if you're right-handed) is the same as a matched grip. For the left hand, place the stick in the bottom of the "V" between your thumb and index finger and lightly squeeze together. This is the fulcrum for your left hand. Remember that the fulcrum is where you hold and control the stick—do not squeeze too hard: stay relaxed. The stick will rest on the ring finger with your pinky underneath for support. Wrap your index finger over the stick and keep the thumb close to it. Sometimes they touch and sometimes they don't, depending on your finger movement while playing. The middle finger is a guide and is also used with reverse-finger technique.

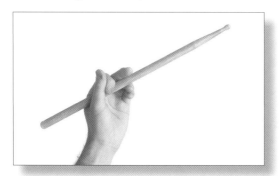

For both grips you can loosen your fulcrum (i.e., let go) to get a looser sound. Don't be afraid to drop a stick. If you do, just relax, reach down and grab a new one from your stick bag while you're still playing. With a matched grip you can also let go of your fulcrum in both hands and control the sticks with your fingers under the stick. This works well when you're playing loud and bashing. Experiment with where your fulcrum will be on the stick. Sometimes you'll grip up higher on the stick and other times you might grip way down and use more of the stick. This all depends on the style of music you're playing. Find a grip that feels right for you and then experiment with alternate grips.

GROOVE

What defines the groove in a song? I like to keep it simple. You walk into a club or concert, and as you start to hear the band, something physically attacks your being. The vibe of the song along with the beat and togetherness of the band is so deep that it makes the hair on the back of your neck stand up. Your overall feeling is to move or dance, to feel the beat and just let go. That's *groove*. When you're behind the drumset and you're making that groove happen with the rest of the rhythm section, and you're locked in to the groove as a single entity, you are in the zone of the *groove* (sometimes called "channeling"). You don't want it to stop. The term "groove" is also used as a slang word in everyday life. If you ask a musician "How was your vacation?" he or she might respond, "It was a groove." By that response, you know it was a great trip. I once asked Jeff Porcaro how he was doing and he answered, "I'm just trying to catch one [a groove]." I thought that said it all. One time when I was in the studio with Jeff working on a record, I noticed that when we were listening back to a take he was marking time with his fist on the drum baffle in half time to the track he just played. He did this all the way through the song. When it was done he looked at me and said, "Mark this take. This one grooves the hardest." From that moment on, I knew that was one thing he did when he played to get that big wide fat time-feel. His body would be feeling half time while he was playing in double time. He was the master of groove. When he walked into a room, the room changed because of his groove.

Where does the groove come from? According to many African drum masters, it comes from the earth and travels upward through our bodies. You have to be open and willing to accept the groove. It lies in the big notes—the whole notes, half notes, and quarter notes—the big open ostinatos that ground your body to the earth. It's because of the grounding of the big notes that you can play and groove the more syncopated and faster rhythms over the foundation that you've established on the bottom. Some people are just born with the groove. Others have to work harder at finding it, but come to it in time. Some deny it their whole lives.

Committing to the groove is the biggest decision you'll ever make before you count off a song as a drummer. You don't want to sound like you're searching for the groove during the first four bars, or anywhere in the song for that matter. Define what you want to play before you play it and commit to it. Keep it simple, stay in the pocket with the bass player, and don't step on the melody. Remember, it's not *what* you play, but *how* you play what you play. Your groove separates you from everyone else. It's the most important thing that you can work on. It's not how fast you can play, but how deep you can groove. It defines who you are as a drummer. Groove can only happen on the bandstand or in the studio if everyone gets it. It doesn't always happen and can never be taken for granted. When it's right, and you're not thinking about it, that's when the magic happens. There is an old saying, "If you're playing and thinking about groovin', you're probably not."

Track 30 demonstrates one of an infinite number of possible grooves. Listen to it carefully and try to *feel* the groove, but don't think about it.

TRACK 30

Always listen, feel, and let your body be open to the groove; it is a reaction to an emotional response that lives within your soul.

GOSPEL

Gospel is a form of black American music that literally translates into "good news," from the Old English "god-spell," as translated from and used in the New Testament.

Gospel music appeared alongside the rise of the Pentecostal church worship services in the late nineteenth century. Influenced by spiritual and blues singing, the style is characterized by dominant lead vocals, large vocal choirs, and lush vocal harmonies. Performance tempos are usually slow to moderate, except with the style known as *shout*, which is extremely fast. A common element of gospel song is the *vamp*, in which a solo singer improvises, often showing the extremes of his/her vocal range over an underlying reiterated phrase sung by a background choir or group.

Folk-related hymns make up the often anonymous repertoire, featuring syncopation and re-accentuation, grand ranges of pitch inflection, harmonizing, and repetitive performance themes such as *call-and-response delivery*. Piano, electric guitar, bass, and drums are the mainstays of the gospel rhythm section.

Gospel music has had a marked influence on rhythm and blues and soul music, which have in turn significantly guided contemporary gospel music. Other resulting genres include urban contemporary and modern gospel, known as "contemporary Christian."

TRACK 31

The following example has an upbeat two-beat feel. This is much harder to play steadily at faster tempos. Take your time and work on this groove at slower tempos and then gradually increase the tempo.

The following are a few well-established gospel artists. Listen to their recordings to absorb a sampling of the gospel sound.

- Andraé Crouch
- Aretha Franklin
- Mahalia Jackson
- BeBe & CeCe Winans
- Aaron Neville
- Take 6

Remember to saturate yourself with as much music as you can in the style on which you're working.

GOALS

The first step to accomplishing your goals is to put them down on paper. As you achieve your goals, cross them off your list and add new goals. For example, my goal is to finish this book by the due date, so I write the date down and get on a schedule. I also write the schedule down on paper, stick to it, and finish. I've now accomplished my goal and met my deadline.

Everyone should have short-and long-term goals. Set goals for practicing, business, networking, where you want to be in your career, and what you want to accomplish in your personal life. A balanced life makes you a stronger artist. I'm a firm believer in writing things down. It frees the mind up to be creative. It also enables you to look back in time and see what you have or have not accomplished. From there you can make adjustments. It's a good check-and-balance system that works.

Make a list of your short- and long-term goals. Then, write down a schedule, stick with your plan, and achieve your goals. Go for it!

HI-HAT

The hi-hat consists of two cymbals that are pedal-operated. These two cymbals are generally 13" to 15" in diameter. Although sizes and weights can vary, the lower cymbal is fixed and is most often heavier than the top one. Both are threaded onto a hollow metal shaft, which contains a clutch that runs from the top cymbal into the foot pedal. When the foot pedal is depressed, the upper cymbal is lowered, and when the two meet, they are "choked" together.

Drummers play the hi-hat in many different ways depending on the desired effect. This includes striking the hi-hat when it's open, closed, or in positions anywhere in between. A drumstick can be used to strike the cymbals, or the foot pedal can be manipulated to bring the two cymbals together, creating a splashy sound. The most common sound created with the foot pedal is a "chicking" produced when the pedal is pressed down.

TRACK 32

On **Track 32**, a pair of 14" medium-light Paiste hi-hat cymbals is being played in a jazz swing feel. Listen to the different sounds of the hi-hat .

When you pick out a pair of hi-hats, make sure that you play them with the rest of your cymbals on the drumset so that you can hear and feel how they blend together. Always use the sticks that you will be playing with in the style. Have someone else play the hi-hats while you step back and listen. This way you can hear how they sound and blend with the drumset and your other cymbals in the room.

The following photos show all types of hi-hat sets used on the CD with this book.

15" Alpha Rock hi-hats: Paiste

Giant beat hi-hats: Paiste

15" Dark Energy hi-hats: Paiste

13" Dimensions hi-hats: Paiste

14" Traditional medium light hi-hats: Paiste

HEADS

A membrane made of parchment, plastic, or animal skin can serve as the head of a drum. The drumhead is struck with the bare hand or stick-like percussive tools to cause vibrations that result in an emanating resonant sound.

Cultures around the world originally used animal skin as their preferred material for the drumhead. The plastic drumhead was not introduced until 1956, along with those crafted of polyester. These man-made versions quickly gained (and have maintained) popularity as they were categorically more durable, more affordable, and less affected by changes in climate and weather than the more traditional animal skin heads.

Hand drums such as congas, frame drums, and djembes are more likely to make use of animal skins, but plastic heads are also used for hand drums. Remo World Percussion instruments offer a wide variety of plastic-head drums complete with tuning keys. Kevlar, a manmade fiber, is another material commonly used for drumheads, preferred in situations such as marching percussion for its unsurpassed durability and resilience under great tension.

Take your time and experiment with a variety of heads for your drumset(s) and hand drums. Different combinations, weights, and tunings make a huge difference in sound.

HEAD COMBINATIONS

Bass Drum Head Combinations

The following are my favorite head combinations, all of which are used on the accompanying CD.

Remo Power Stroke 3 Batter

> 22" Power Stroke 3 batter and Ambassador resonant (Remo); for rock, funk, and pop.

> 20" Pinstripe Coated batter and Ambassador resonant (Remo); for funk, hip-hop, and Latin.

> 18" Fiberskyn 3, Ambassador batter and resonant (Remo); wide open tune to a note, for jazz, light funk, and hip-hop.

Tom Combinations

> Any size tom: Coated Ambassador (Remo) top and bottom; for studio, live, pop, rock, and funk.

> Any size tom: Coated Ambassador (Remo) top, Clear Diplomats (Remo) bottom, more ring; for studio, pop, rock, funk, and jazz.

> Any size tom: Fiberskyn 3 Ambassador (Remo) top and bottom, more ring; for studio, live, jazz, and light pop.

> Any size tom: Coated Emperor (Remo) top and Ambassador Coated (Remo) bottom (tuned tighter than the top head); creates a nice open rock sound (John Bonham).

Coated Emperor (Remo)

Snare

Any size snare: Coated Ambassador (Remo) top and Resonant (Remo) bottom—my favorite snare sound.

World Percussion hand drums, Djembes, Bongos, Tubanos, Djun-Djuns, etc.: Fiberskyn 3 World Percussion Heads (Remo) or Nuskyn World Percussion Heads (Remo).

Coated Ambassador (Remo)

Nuskyn: Bongo (Remo)

Nuskyn: Conga (Remo)

Nuskyn: Taiko (Remo)

Nuskyn: Tubano (Remo)

HIP-HOP

The term "hip-hop" comes from a lifestyle referring to culture, graffiti, break dancing, and rapping, with turntable scratching surrounding the music. Once rap had been established and had history, hip-hop looked back to the old regime of artists including MCs like Kurtis Blow and Whodini, and DJs like Grand Master Flash and Afrika Bambaataa. Hip-hop is the culture from which rap emerged, and it has its own language, style of dress, music, and state of mind that is constantly changing.

Listen to the following recommended artists:

- Afrika Bambaataa
- Ice Cube
- Will Smith
- LL Cool J
- Beastie Boys
- Dr. Dre
- DMX
- Kurtis Blow
- Coolio
- Queen Latifah
- Eminem
- Timbaland

G-funk is the lazy, behind the beat, Parliament/Funkadelic-influenced variation of "gangsta rap" created by Dr. Dre in the early '90s. Low-end bass grooves along with synths, slow programmed drumbeats, and oftentimes generic female backup vocals. G-funk became the most popular sub-genre of hip-hop in the early '90s. After the success of Dr. Dre's 1992 album, *The Chronic* (the CD in which he invented and named the style), Dr. Dre opened the door and influenced many new rap artists and producers who used his musical techniques to make a recognizable sound in rap for most of the early '90s.

The following list includes a few recommended artists/albums. Pay attention to the rhythms and rhymes of the raps and the programmed drum and bass grooves.

- Dr. Dre: *2001*
- Snoop Doggy Dogg: *The Last Meal*
- Ice Cube: *The Predator*
- Snoop Doggy Dogg: *The Doggfather*
- Tupac Shakur: *Me Against the World*

Alternative/underground hip-hop exists as an attempt to reflect what is believed by certain artists to be the original elements of the culture. Artists such as Talib Kweli, Mos Def, Dilated

Peoples, Dead Prez, Blackalicious, and Jurassic 5 may emphasize messages of verbal skill, unity, or activism, instead of messages of violence, material wealth, and misogyny.

Track 33 is a real-time hip-hop groove with a swingin' hi-hat (swing sixteenths). The bass drum is an old vintage Slingerland 18" bass drum with two Fiberskyn 3 heads, wide open with no dampening. It almost has a Roland TR-808 drum machine sound to it. The bass drum part is very simple with a lot of space. The lope of the groove is in the hi-hat.

Examples A–P below are similar beats to **Track 33**. Experiment with them, and then write some of your own grooves. Remember to include the slightly swung sixteenth-note feel.

TRACK 33

With all the drum programming and sequencing over the last twenty years, we have begun to experience different time-feels. In order to relate to the programmed beats and grooves that we hear, we must make adjustments in our time-feel. Sometimes the groove is swinging in the middle of straight eighths and swing time, which is known as "using different increments of swing." There is no right or wrong in this process. You just have to find that spot that feels good and make the song feel right. If you are programming grooves using sequencing software, you will be able to select your *quantization* (time correction to nearest beat chosen) as well as your different increments of swing such as straight eighths, triplets, or sixteenth notes. You can experiment with the programmed groove by adjusting the quantization until it feels right to you in the track. We must do this when we play as well—find that spot in the time-feel that makes the track happen between the bass drum, hi-hat, and snare.

HEAVY METAL

"Heavy metal" (or simply "metal") refers to a sub-genre of hard rock music that was developed in the late '60s and early '70s. Key elements include virtuosic and intense performances of fast soloing, distorted electric guitar, predominant use of power chords, wailing vocals, and double bass drumming. Metal springs from a group of related styles, the dominant being that of blues-rock, and to a lesser degree, psychedelic rock. Seminal figures in the evolution of metal include Jimi Hendrix, Led Zeppelin, Deep Purple, and Black Sabbath. Leading a revival in the early 1980s-'90s were Metallica, Guns N' Roses, and in the '90s, Nirvana.

In the beginning, double bass drum technique was made popular by drummers such as Louie Bellson, Keith Moon, Ginger Baker, and Billy Cobham. Drummers used two bass drums with two pedals. Today, you have a choice of using two bass drums or a double bass drum pedal attached to one bass drum. Double bass drum technique can be used to drive the bottom end of the band, increase the intensity of a song as it builds between sections, or for syncopated bass drum patterns that are too fast to play with one bass drum. Double bass drum playing is very popular in heavy metal today.

The following list includes hard rock bands that influenced heavy metal or were considered heavy metal in their time (1967-1979). Listen to these bands, focusing on the drummers in this style.

- AC/DC (Phil Rudd)
- Cream (Ginger Baker)
- Deep Purple (Ian Paice)
- Iron Butterfly (Ron Bushy)
- Judas Priest (Simon Phillips, Scott Travis)
- Led Zeppelin (John Bonham)
- Rush (Neil Peart)
- Van Halen (Alex Van Halen)
- Vanilla Fudge (Carmine Appice)
- Uriah Heep (Lee Kerslake)
- Black Sabbath (Cozy Powell, Vinny Appice, and Bill Ward)

The next list includes a few heavy metal bands that were influenced by the older hard rock bands.

- System of a Down (John Dolmayan)
- Primus (Tim "Herb" Alexander)
- Mötley Crüe (Tommy Lee)
- Slayer (Dave Lombardo)
- Metallica (Lars Ulrich)
- Megadeth (Shawn Drover)
- Motörhead (Mikkey Dee)

Track 34 is a heavy metal-type groove utilizing double bass drum. Examples A–D display several similar grooves. Work on these beats and then come up with some of your own grooves in the style. For more information on this subject, see my book *Rock Drumming Workbook* (Hal Leonard).

TRACK 34

(splashy hi-hat)

HALF-TIME FEEL

In 4/4 time, placing the backbeat on beat 3
(instead of on beats 2 and 4) creates a half-time feel.

Example B features a half-time funk shuffle groove played in an eight-bar phrase. The strong
backbeat is on beat 3. The non-accented snare-drum notes are *ghost notes* (softer notes).
The ghost notes help the groove to fill in and create forward motion in the time-feel. Go to
Swing Feel (p. 106) and check out the triplet exercise. This will help you with the half-time
shuffle feel.

TRACK 35

Play 3 times:
Fade out on 3rd time

Work on these grooves and write some of your own half-time beats in different styles. Also check out Bernard Purdie on Steely Dan's song "Home at Last" from the *AJA* album, and Jeff Porcaro on "Rosanna" from Toto's *Toto IV* album.

HARD ROCK

Hard rock is a sub-genre of rock 'n' roll music. Its origins can be traced back to garage and psychedelic rock bands of the early 1960s like Deep Purple and Black Sabbath. These bands played a darker, blues-influenced style of rock with heavy distorted guitars, drums, and bass, favoring power chords and sometimes dissonant angular riffs.

Notable hard rock bands with beginnings in the '60s and '70s include:

- AC/DC (Phil Rudd)
- Cream (Ginger Baker)
- Deep Purple (Ian Paice)
- Iron Butterfly (Ron Bushy)
- Judas Priest (Simon Phillips, Scott Travis)
- Led Zeppelin (John Bonham)
- Rush (Neil Peart)
- Van Halen (Alex Van Halen)
- Vanilla Fudge (Carmine Appice)
- Uriah Heep (Lee Kerslake)
- Black Sabbath (Billy Ward)

In the latter part of the hard rock era, beginning in the early 1990s, bands like Metallica and Guns N' Roses became wildly popular. They dominated the charts at that time with their multi-platinum record releases. In 1992, a new form of rock emerged known as grunge, featuring effects such as heavy use of feedback and fuzzy distorted guitar. Bands such as Pearl Jam, Nirvana, Soundgarden, and Alice in Chains became very popular in the grunge era. Listen to these bands to hear some of the most prominent drummers in this style.

Track 36 demonstrates two feels in a full-band rock context. Example A shows the 4/4 section, which has a strong straight-eighth rock feel, with a splashy hi-hat accenting the quarter notes à la John Bonham (Led Zeppelin). The groove has a big, fat, laid back open sound. Example B features a 6/8 rock feel (you'll hear this change towards the end of **Track 36**). The 6/8 meter signifies six beats per measure with the eighth note getting the beat.

TRACK 36

Practice playing Example A, going directly into Example B to get used to the change of feels. Remember that the eighth note stays constant coming from the 4/4 section. Also practice going back to the 4/4 feel from the 6/8 groove. For more information on this subject, see my book *Rock Drumming Workbook* (Hal Leonard).

Examples C and D feature two additional contrasting grooves, one in 4/4, and one in 6/8. Practice going smoothly back and forth between the two.

HANDS

Even if you're not a hand-drum player, spend some time at the drumset playing with your hands. Using your hands and fingers will give you a completely different dynamic sound and feel on the kit. Try to play rudiments, grooves, fills, and solo ideas. You can substitute your hands for brushes to play softly, and then pick up sticks when you need to change into a louder sound. Also experiment with playing a shaker in your right hand, with your left hand playing the snare drum against the bass drum and hi-hat.

Track 37 demonstrates a funky samba feel with hands only (no sticks). Have fun creating new sounds on the drumset. Think outside the box.

TRACK 37

INTERNAL CLOCK

Your inner time clock is the means by which you feel time without reference to an external click. The first way to work on your time-feel is to develop your internal clock. Count yourself in and play a groove at any tempo for three to five minutes. Record yourself and listen back to see how steady the time was from beginning to end. Repeat the same procedure when you are rehearsing or on a gig with your band. This will make you aware of your internal clock. Ask yourself: Am I rushing, slowing down, or in the pocket? Is the bass player pushing or dragging the time?

The stronger your inner clock is, the more people will want to lean on your time-feel and groove with you. Keep in mind that your internal clock is not a drum machine—it does not have perfect time. When you are playing with your internal clock (versus with a click, sequence tracks, or loops), the time-feel should breathe. Work on all your grooves, fills, and phrasing ideas at different tempos to develop a strong internal clock. One, two, three, four, go!

INFLUENCE

Being influenced by great drummers throughout history is something we should all focus on. Learning grooves, fills, and solo ideas from the drummers who speak to us is an incredible, ongoing learning experience. Once you learn a signature groove from a drummer that you're groovin' on, start to experiment with morphing that groove into something new that is your own. When you listen to other people play, be open to receive the groove. Let it wash over you. It will come out in your playing in a new way down the road. Remember that your time-feel is a living, breathing thing that is unique to you. That's why we can all play the same groove, but we will all sound different. So keep your ears open, and listen for and learn new beats, fills, and ideas from all the drummers that you love. This is how you will come up with your signature grooves, fills, and solo ideas.

INDEPENDENCE

As drummers, we are always working on the independence of our limbs. It doesn't matter what the style of music is, your two- or four-way coordination is always being challenged as you bring new ideas into your playing. In the next example, the feel is made up of a jazz ride cymbal against syncopated upbeat and downbeat triplets on the snare and bass drum.

TRACK 38

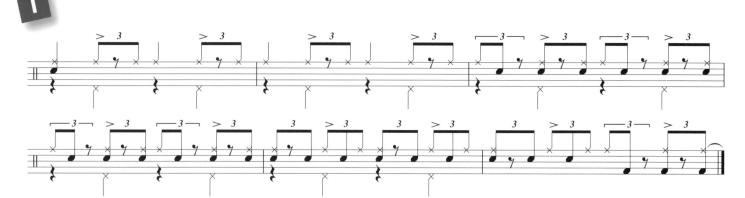

Write some of your own independence exercises in different styles. For more information on this subject, check out my book *Drummer's Guide to Odd Meters* as well as *In the Pocket* by John Snider and *Afro-Cuban Coordination for the Drumset* by Maria Martinez (all published by Hal Leonard).

INTERACTION

Interaction with other musicians is a must in establishing a strong inner time-feel. Staring at a computer all day or staying in your practice room by yourself is no way to learn to groove and establish relationships with people. You should try to balance your time between practicing and playing alone (play-alongs, etc.), and making music with others. Other musicians to play with include other drummers and percussionists, bass players, full rhythm sections (start your own band), and larger ensembles of any nature (school jazz band, percussion ensemble, concert band, or marching band). If you're out of school, try to get into a rehearsal band or go down to your local club and try to sit in. Working out parts together and making time-feel adjustments with the other musicians is crucial to your development as a drummer. Remember, music is about the interaction between people getting together and trying to make a statement. So, take a risk and interact.

IMPROVISE

To be able to improvise freely on the drumset you need to have a solid rhythmic vocabulary. It's like having all your rhythmic knowledge in a giant database, and you pull things out as needed in different orders as you react to the musical style and song form that you're playing. You can't improvise without a vocabulary. Sometimes you really surprise yourself, and sometimes you don't. Work on phrasing two-, four-, eight-, twelve-, and sixteen-bar phrases.

See *Rhythmic Guide* (p. 96) and Step 4 in the *Five Steps to Musicality* (p. 42) for more detailed information that will help you with your improvisation and soloing. To get started, listen to the following great improvisers from past and present:

- Charlie Parker (alto sax)
- John Coltrane (tenor and soprano sax)
- Miles Davis (trumpet)
- Herbie Hancock (piano)
- Chick Corea (piano)
- Mike Stern (guitar)
- Ron Escheté (guitar)
- Bill Evans (piano)

- Elvin Jones (drums)
- Philly Joe Jones (drums)
- Buddy Rich (drums)
- Art Blakey (drums)
- Tony Williams (drums)
- Steve Gadd (drums)
- Max Roach (drums)
- Keith Moon (drums)

Track 39 is a jazzy march improv. A four-bar phrase is repeated as I improvise off the march groove. This was the first take with no click. After you do some listening, record yourself playing over different phrase lengths and forms in different styles.

TRACK 39

JAZZ

Jazz is a musical form based on improvisation and rooted in the blues. It was developed from African American rhythms and influenced by European harmonic structure. There is much debate on the subject, but it is generally agreed that jazz developed predominantly in New Orleans beginning in the late nineteenth century. During those early years, jazz was greatly influenced by a combination of ragtime and blues. One of the first great jazz soloists, Louis Armstrong, paved the way for the era of swing (1930 to 1945) with his rich vocalizations and improvised trumpet playing. By the early 1930s, pianist and bandleader Duke Ellington was introducing elements of both composed and improvised jazz. Duke was followed by 1940s be-bop innovators like saxophonist Charlie Parker and trumpeter Dizzy Gillespie. Parker and Gillespie pioneered the new course for improvising over chord changes.

Trumpeter Miles Davis is particularly known for establishing a relaxed cool jazz movement in the 1950s, and for the funk, rock, and electronic elements that he brought into his music. It is said that Miles changed the direction of jazz music five times. In the 1960s, saxophonist John Coltrane explored new directions by extending the chord progressions of be-bop, along with his experimental stages of improvisation. To this day, the exploratory art form of jazz is a driving global force.

Listen to the following jazz artists, which represent some of the most notable modern innovators of the genre:

- Art Blakey (drums)
- Dave Brubeck (piano)
- John Coltrane (tenor and soprano sax)
- Chick Corea (piano)
- Miles Davis (trumpet)
- Bill Evans (piano)
- Gil Evans (arranger)
- Steve Gadd (drums)
- Dizzy Gillespie (trumpet)
- Herbie Hancock (piano)
- Elvin Jones (drums)

- Philly Joe Jones (drums)
- Pat Metheny (guitar)
- Charles Mingus (bass)
- Thelonious Monk (piano)
- Charlie Parker (alto sax)
- Bud Powell (piano)
- Max Roach (drums)
- Sonny Rollins (tenor sax)
- Mike Stern (guitar)
- Tony Williams (drums)

The next example represents one of many possible jazz forms. The intro is six bars and has a two feel. Letter A is eight bars, B is eight bars, and C is twelve bars. A, B, and C are straight-ahead swing, but you should also work on playing different jazz feels over a twelve-bar blues and thirty-two-bar song forms.

TRACK 40

The next example is a short jazz phrasing idea. Though the meter is 4/4, the phrasing can be divided up (as the dotted bar lines show) into two measures of 3/4, and one measure of 2/4. This creates a 3/4 feel over the bar line. Practice this, and then use your own creativity to come up with similar jazz phrasing ideas.

Additional jazz idea

KICK DRUM

The kick drum (or bass drum) is the largest and deepest-sounding drum in the orchestra, and the heartbeat of the drumset. The drumset player strikes the kick drum by depressing a foot pedal attached to a bass drum beater. Kick drums are tuned with a proposed style of music in mind. For example, to get a rock sound, the tuning should be low, flat, and punchy, whereas higher, more open-pitched tuning may be appropriate for playing jazz. The size of a kick drum usually ranges from 16" to 24" in diameter with a depth of 14" to 18".

Two other types of bass drums are the pitched bass and the concert bass. The pitched bass drum is most commonly used in marching bands and drum corps, where it is played with one or two large mallets. These drums are usually seen in a section of three to six bass drums. The concert bass drum is a pitched bass drum that is played with a large fluffy mallet. This drum is usually heard in orchestral music and concert bands and is the largest drum in the orchestra.

TRACK 41

Track 41 demonstrates three different exposed bass drums that make up the bottom end of a programmed loop. They are an attack bass drum (22" Pacific LX sample), a sonic bass drum (sample) and a house bass drum (sample). This loop was sequenced in Logic. Sometimes I like to use more than one bass drum sound in the track to add different dynamic levels and tone colors.

Remember, when you choose a bass drum for recording or for playing live, make sure the size of the drum and the head combinations fit the vibe of the music. Experiment with different bass drums and head combinations. For more information, see *Heads* (p. 54).

Below are the different bass drums used on this CD.

18" x 14" Vintage Slingerland (wide open)

20" x 18" Pacific LX (with pillow)

22" x 18" Pacific LX (with pillow)

22" x 18" Pacific CX (lower tuning, with pillow and padding)

22" x 18" Pacific CX

LISTEN

Developing your listening skills and your ears is one of the most important things you will do as a musician. This is a lifelong process.

The next time you listen to a song, first listen to the drums; then spend some time dissecting the rest of the band's parts. Start by learning the bass player's part. Learn it and sing it out loud while you play along on the kit. Check out how the bass part works with the drum groove. Repeat this process with the other parts—guitars, keyboards, horns, melody instruments, and vocals—one at a time. After you've experimented with this process for a month, the next time you play with a band, see if you're hearing more of the song and interacting better with the band. Record yourself at rehearsals and gigs and monitor your progress. Remember to saturate yourself in the style that you are working on by doing a lot of listening. This will improve your rhythmic, harmonic, and melodic vocabulary. Do not stay in a bubble surrounding the drumset. Get your ears out into the room so you can hear everything you need to hear live, or in your headphone mix, so you can react and play musically in every situation. Always play for the song and remember that the melody rules the show. Do not step on the melody or overplay.

When you're working, you also have to listen and take notes for chart changes and cues from the leader or conductor. Keep your eyes and ears open so you always know the road map of the song. Keep listening and you will develop "big ears!"

LOPE (OF THE GROOVE)

The *lope* is the dynamic and forward motion of the groove. The lope of the groove on the drumset usually happens on the hi-hat or ride cymbal. Musicians explain this process in different ways. Think of an egg rolling end-over-end on a table; it would not be a perfect roll. Creating dynamic and accent changes within one or two bars of the groove is how you create the lope.

TRACK 42

Track 42 features a half-time groove in which the hi-hat has a skipping forward motion lope, while the snare and bass drum are centered. Spend some time finding the lope of the groove in your beats. For more on this subject, check out Jeff Porcaro's *Instructional DVD for Drums* (Hal Leonard).

LOOPS

A loop is a beat or musical phrase (usually one or two bars in length) that is copied electronically, and repeated over and over. The beat is usually grabbed (edited) from a longer real-time recorded performance or a programmed beat.

The way drummers work these days has changed drastically compared to the pre-MIDI days. Let's look back for a moment and appreciate the changes. Before 1981, every drum track was recorded with a live drummer. Recording with a live rhythm section (drums, bass, guitar, and piano) was the way to track at recording sessions. Then the Linn Drum LM1 and Linn Drum 2 came out, which changed everything.

Drum machine-driven tracks became the norm during the eighties. Everyone was programming beats for records, films, television, and jingles. It became the new sound that everyone wanted. It also made anyone with good rhythmic ideas consider themselves a drummer and/or percussionist in the studio. In the '90s, the alternative rock scene hit and the sound of live rhythm sections returned. But at the same time, rap and hip-hop started to explode with programmed drumbeats and drum loops.

So, here we are in 2007 and drum loops are bigger than ever. Let's get started using some simple ways to create a library of your own drum and percussion loops.

The next time you're in a studio, recording with your band or doing a session for someone, ask the engineer if he would record you while he is getting drum sounds. After you do all the individual hits on the drums, cymbals, etc. (which will be very useful to you to load into your sampler software), it will be time to play the whole kit. At this time you should be prepared to play grooves at the tempos you want that you can later load into your audio recording software or a digital audio workstation. You can then cut up your loops and do edits. This will get you started recording loops of your own. If you don't have your own studio, you can get together with someone later who can edit the loops for you and burn them onto a CD. You will now have a library of loops that you can use when you work for songwriters and producers, or for your own compositions.

Make sure you keep good records of your loops. Notate tempo, style, and time-feel. Mix the drumsets up and use different sizes for different styles. For example, you might have some rock loops played with larger-sized drums, 22" or 24" bass drums; 13", 14", or 16" toms; and larger cymbals. Or you could record some funk and hip-hop grooves with a 20" bass drum; and 10", 12", and 14" toms. Or use a jazz kit with an 18" bass drum, and 12" and 14" toms. Make a point to mix and match sets and head combinations. Try to get different sounds for different styles. Also use different-sized snare drums and cymbals.

Track 43 is a programmed loop made in the audio recording software Logic. Each part was played into the software using a keyboard controller. The hi-hat track was run through the pitch bend wheel of the controller to achieve the weird pitch changes. It's a big open groove.

TRACK 43

The next loop has a slower, looser hip-hop feel. This full mix performance loop starts out with a 22" bass drum, 14" Bronze snare (Pacific), and splashy 14" Signature hi-hats (Paiste). Groovers (Regal Tip) are the sticks used on this track. A CANZ shaker (Rhythm Tech) was overdubbed. Example A shows this loop in notation.

TRACK 44

A Loops

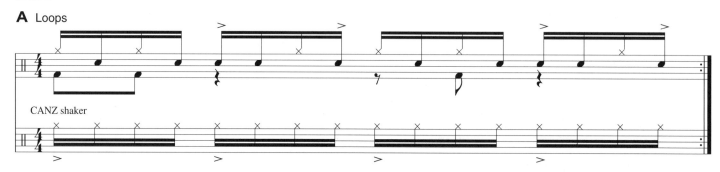

Example B shows the next loop, which uses an old 18" vintage bass drum (Slingerland) wide open with Fiberskyn 3 heads (Remo) on the front and back of the drum, with no muffling. The snare is a 10" Popcorn snare (Pacific) with a Fiberskyn head. The track also showcases timbale sticks (Regal Tip) playing the drumset, along with the top of the bass drum being played with my right hand to get that woody clicking sound. I clicked quarter notes with my left foot on the 14" Signature Series hi-hat (Paiste), and overdubbed the cowbell.

B Right hand plays bass drum rim (notated in space above the staff)

Cowbell

Have fun creating your own drum and percussion loops. For more information on this topic, check out my book/CD *Creating Professional Drum Loops* (Amsco Publications, Music Sales Group).

LIVE PERFORMANCE

Performing live as a drummer takes a lot of energy. When you are onstage playing a concert in a large theater or arena, it can be very hot under the lights—a far cry from being in an air-conditioned studio. I've played shows in Vegas that consisted of three hours of nonstop drumming. You have to pace yourself and stay relaxed. If you're playing a long show, make sure you have plenty of water with you to stay hydrated.

Practice at different dynamic levels and tempos, as well as in different styles, so you will be prepared for anything under any conditions. Make sure your equipment is in good shape and that you always have extra pedals, heads, hardware, and sticks with you close at hand.

I remember playing a concert with an audience of 20,000 when my foot pedal broke in half on the downbeat of the first song. Luckily, I had an extra pedal right under my floor tom, so I played time on the floor tom and snare until the drum tech ran onto the stage and replaced the pedal.

Remember, live is live. There are no second takes. Be prepared for anything!

LATIN

The term "Latin" is often used to refer to numerous musical styles from Cuba, Puerto Rico, the Caribbean, Spain, Mexico, and South America.

The reason the general term "Latin" is used here rather than specifying a particular Latin style is due to the fact that many charts will indicate something like "Latin, straight eighths" as a tempo/style direction. Such a chart could be 4/4 and have a 4/4 feel, not a two-feel like samba.

The next few examples feature several Latin grooves. Example A demonstrates the kind of groove I usually start off with when I see a chart like the one mentioned above. This groove features a driving rhythm with a quarter-note side stick that works well with most bass lines and can also be used during B sections of bossa novas. Example B features a triplet pattern played on the ride, and Example C goes into a double-time feel on the ride. **Track 46** features a groove that combines all three of these beats (Note: the track does not play exactly what is notated in examples A–C). At the end of the track, the rhythm is broken up between the hands, and it's more syncopated for the last three bars or so. Practice these grooves, as it is likely you will find much use for them.

A Latin feel

B (Play ride with a triplet feel)

C

METER

Meter is the organized grouping of musical rhythms; it is the rhythm of the phrase, not of the measure.

The East Indian tabla masters have an incredible sense of meter. They usually play in 4/4 time and superimpose odd meter subdivisions over 4/4 while they sing the tones they are playing. Their phrases are long stories and they play over and through the bar lines as if there were not any. Their use of meter within these long phrases separates their sound from that of music originating in the West, which, in its notation, typically focuses on playing within the bar lines, not over and through the bar lines. For more information, see *Over and Through the Bar Line* (p. 82).

One can look at meter within longer phrases as if driving a car with a stick shift—sometimes you're just cruising along and not shifting gears as fast. Other times you downshift to slow down, and still other times you upshift to speed up. As drummers, we do this over an underlying pulse or *ostinato* (repeated phrase) unless the tempo is *rubato* (stolen or free time), or a tempo change occurs. Either way, we are establishing our meter within the given phrase.

A poet establishes his/her meter in long and short syllables in verse. We do the same when we play the drums. Consider this the next time you sit down to play.

MAINTENANCE

Drum maintenance is something all drummers need to do. It doesn't matter whether you do it yourself, or someone does it for you, as long as it gets done. When you're not working, try to take care of specific things that are wrong with your kit, such as changing heads, oiling pedals, and changing snare wires and cymbal felts.

But usually things go wrong at the worst possible time. Be prepared for anything, especially if you do not have a drum tech maintaining your gear. Make sure you have the following supplies with you at all times:

Maintenance list

- Spare heads (always!)
- Duct tape for muffling drums
- Screwdrivers—Flathead and Phillips, large and small
- Allen wrenches and pliers
- Spare cymbal felts, nylon cymbal sleeves, and wing nuts
- Extra foot pedal and hi-hat stand
- WD-40 for squeaky pedals
- Drum keys
- Snare string or plastic strap
- Extra hi-hat clutch
- Pencils (to mark charts)
- Earplugs
- Extra bass drum beaters

MARCH

A march is a composition of well-marked rhythm suitable for marching; generally in 2/4, 6/8, or *Alla breve* (4/4 counted as 2/2) meter.

The next example is a funky march feel in 4/4 time, played in four-bar phrases. Only four bars have been notated so you can check out the orchestration, but **Track 47** plays a longer example.

TRACK 47

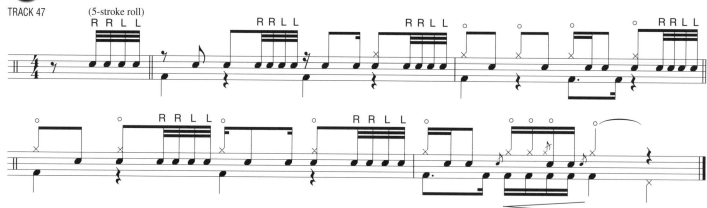

Learn this example (the first four bars), and then write out the rest of **Track 47** and learn the whole piece. Once you have that under your belt, write a funky march cadence of your own for drumset.

Check out *Rudiments* (p. 92). These will help you big-time with your marches, especially the five-, six-, and seven-stroke rolls. Once you get a feel for the march you want to play and decide on the sticking and tempo, you can start to stylize the feel and apply it to the whole drumset.

It is recommended that you work on rudiments with a teacher. Once you learn them on the snare drum, a good instructor can help you apply them to the drumset, setting them in the context of different styles. For more information on this subject, check out the book/CD *Rudimental Warm-ups* by Maria Martinez (Hal Leonard) and Joe Porcaro's *Drum Set Method* (JoPo Music Publications).

MOTOWN

Motown was a Detroit-based record company that became synonymous with its own distinctive style of black soul music, which grew hugely popular in the 1960s. Songwriter Berry Gordy founded the Motown record company, training all the songwriters and musicians in what became the label's signature musical style. In an attempt to reach both black and white audiences, Motown quickly spawned nationwide hit-makers, including Smokey Robinson and the Miracles, and the Marvelettes.

The Funk Brothers

Gordy's distinctive sound came from using not only the same team of songwriters and producers, but a tight group of studio musicians known as "The Funk Brothers" to record the Motown rhythm-section tracks. This famous rhythm section included percussionists Eddie "Bongo" Brown and Jack Ashford, and drummers Benny Benjamin, Uriel Jones, and Richard "Pistol" Allen. The sound had a number of general characteristics with slight variation among artists. Production tended to showcase the lead singer, favoring the high end of the sound register with lyrics that were rich in metaphor and rhyme, and the songs themselves had multiple hooks. "The Funk Brothers" were instrumental in building one of the most successful black-owned businesses in U.S. history, not to mention a hugely influential independent record label.

Subsequent Motown artists included the Supremes, Marvin Gaye, Stevie Wonder, and the Jackson 5. After moving to Los Angeles in 1971, Motown enjoyed continued success with names including Gladys Knight and the Pips, the Isley Brothers, and Lionel Richie. But with the move, Motown eventually lost some of its focus, and as popular styles evolved, its characteristic sound gave way to popular styles of the time. Motown was finally sold by Berry Gordy to MCA Records in 1988. To this day, the Motown sound continues to influence popular music.

The example on **Track 48** is one of the classic Motown grooves, with four quarter notes on the snare drum played as backbeats. The tambourine is playing sixteenth notes with accents on the quarter notes.

TRACK 48

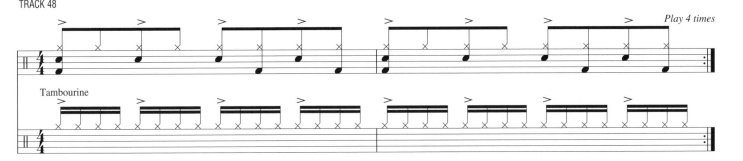

The chart below shows Motown singles that reached number one on the *Billboard* Hot 100 and/or the *Billboard* R&B Singles Chart. There are some classic grooves to listen to on these Motown recordings. Check some of them out and learn from them.

YEAR	TITLE	ARTIST	#1 POP	#1 R&B
1960	Shop Around	The Miracles		1
1961	Please Mr. Postman	The Marvelettes	1	1
1962	Do You Love Me	The Contours		1
1963	(Love Is Like A) Heat Wave	Martha & the Vandellas		1
1964	My Guy	Mary Wells	1	
1964	Baby Love	Supremes	1	
1965	My Girl	Temptations	1	1
1965	I Can't Help Myself (Sugar Pie, Honey Bunch)	Four Tops	1	1
1966	You Can't Hurry Love	Supremes	1	1
1967	I Heard It Through the Grapevine	Gladys Knight & the Pips		1
1968	I Heard It Through the Grapevine	Marvin Gaye	1	1
1969	I Want You Back	Jackson 5	1	1
1970	War	Edwin Starr	1	1
1971	What's Going On	Marvin Gaye		1
1972	Papa Was a Rollin' Stone	Temptations	1	1
1973	Let's Get It On	Marvin Gaye	1	1
1974	Dancing Machine	Jackson 5		1
1977	I Wish	Stevie Wonder	1	1
1980	Upside Down	Diana Ross	1	1
1983	All Night Long (All Night)	Lionel Richie	1	1
1984	I Just Called to Say I Love You	Stevie Wonder	1	1
1985	Rhythm of the Night	DeBarge		1
1993	End of the Road	Boyz II Men	1	
1994	I'll Make Love to You	Boyz II Men	1	1
1997	On & On	Erykah Badu		1
2000	Bag Lady	Erykah Badu		1

MAMBO

The mambo is a ballroom dance and a musical style of Cuban origins, derived from the rumba. "Mambo" was originally a Bantu name given to musical instruments used in rituals, accounting for its translation to "conversation with the gods." Appearing in Cuban ballrooms in the mid-1940s, it posessed elements of swing and other jazz styles. Mambo was made popular in both South and North America by the musician Pérez Prado in the late 1940s, who devised the dance form to accompany and promote his mambo music.

In 1955, the mambo migrated to western Europe and continued to flourish. It is a couples dance, which is accentuated with maracas and claves. The mambo has paved the way for other notable Latin dances such as the cha-cha-cha and the boogaloo.

The following example is a mambo groove written in cut time (2/2). The eight-bar phrase is written without the fill.

TRACK 49

Play 4 times

Mambo Musicians

- Tito Puente
- Pérez Prado
- The Xavier Cugat Orchestra
- Beny Moré
- Arsenio Rodríguez
- Orestes López
- Yma Sumac
- Enrique Jorrín

For more on the mambo, check out *Afro-Cuban Coordination for Drumset* (book/CD and DVD) by Maria Martinez (Hal Leonard).

MIDI

MIDI (musical instrument digital interface) is an industry-standard communications proto-col that allows electronic musical instruments and devices such as computers, keyboards, electronic drums, and other equipment to communicate, control, and synchronize with each other in real time. When MIDI hit the music scene in 1983, the way we worked changed dras-tically. Drum programming became the norm during the '80s with the Linn Drum Machine. I remember doing numerous sessions for TV, film, and records, programming Linn Drum tracks and overdubbing tom fills, or replacing hi-hat and cymbals. The big album that year was *Thriller* by Michael Jackson. The Linn Drum was used on the hit song "Billy Jean."

MIDI does not transmit an audio signal. It simply transmits digital data *event messages*, as opposed to representing actual musical sounds. These messages convey information regard-ing pitch, volume, frequency, vibrato, instrument timbre, note duration, octave designation, and clock signals to set tempo and stopping points in time. A specific sound is created when the data is applied to waveforms that are digitally stored on a computer chip. Despite the advent of more advanced technologies, MIDI has remained virtually unchanged and is used worldwide throughout the industry.

MICROPHONES

A microphone (sometimes referred to as a "mike" or "mic") is an acoustic-to-electric transducer or sensor that converts sound into an electrical signal.

The following is a list of microphones and mic *preamps* (an amplifier that precedes another amplifier for further amplification) that were used to record the CD that accompanies this book. Experiment with different mics, mic "pre's" (preamps), and mic placements. Remember to use your ears and to document combinations that work, feel, and sound good.

Microphones

BD1: SM91 (Shure) • The mic was laid flat on top of the pillow inside the bass drum, which was recorded to a separate track in Pro Tools.

BD2: Beta52A (Shure) • The mic was on a stand just outside the front hole of the bass drum and was recorded to a separate track in Pro Tools. This approach enables you to use either bass drum mike in the mix or combine both mikes to come up with your own bass drum sound.

Snare: SM57 (Shure) • Experiment with this mic position until you like what you hear. Point the mic away from the hi-hat.

Shure Beta52A

Shure SM57

Hi-Hat: SM81 (Shure) • Point the hi-hat mic away from the snare drum.

Tom 1: SM98 Beta (Shure) • These are clip-on mics and should be positioned towards the center of the toms.

Tom 2: SM98 Beta (Shure) • These are clip-on mics and should be positioned towards the center of the toms.

Tom 3: SM98 Beta (Shure) • These are clip-on mics and should be positioned towards the center of the toms.

Popcorn Snare: SM57 (Shure) • Point the mic away from the hi-hat.

Overhead L: KSM32 (Shure) • Experiment with different heights and angles.

Overhead R: KSM32 (Shure) • Experiment with different heights and angles.

Percussion Overdubs: Soundelux E-47

MonoRoom Mike on Drumset: Soundelux E-47 • *Use this track to mix in some room sound when you feel it is appropriate.*

Shure KSM32

Preamps

The Presonus Digimax was used on the following eight channels, recorded optically into Pro Tools at a sampling rate of 44.1: BD 1, BD 2, snare 1, hi-hat, tom 1, tom 2, tom 3, and snare 2.

Overhead Left and Overhead Right: The Great River MP2MV (stereo) mic pre was used on the drums. Overhead channels go into the Avalon 2055EQ, into the Apogee Rosetta 800 (AD) converters, and directly into Pro Tools.

Effects

Use effects sparingly. If you have a stereo audio loop, you don't want to use too much reverb on the drums. Reverb creates space, and if it is recorded on your loops, you can't remove it if it's a stereo loop. I used very little reverb on the CD for that reason. The reverbs used were from the Korg Oasys Card, Digidesign Realverb, and an external Lexicon PCM 60. So be sure to mix things up. Record some loops or tracks completely dry (i.e., no reverb), and then experiment with your effects to come up with new sounds.

NANIGO

Nanigo refers to hybrid grooves/rhythms derived from the percussion instruments that are played for the folkloric Cuban rhythm called *Guiro*, which often accompanies religious ceremonies. Traditionally, the rhythm is played with three or more *shekeres* (beaded gourds) and an iron bell. The drumset has never been part of the traditional 6/8 Afro-Cuban style, but in the Latin-jazz style there are many hybrid interpretations of the 6/8 Afro-Cuban rhythms.

The next examples demonstrate this Cuban rhythm. Example B is a four-bar phrase with three groups of four sixteenth notes in the last bar (three over six). **Track 50** plays Example A going right into Example B.

TRACK 50

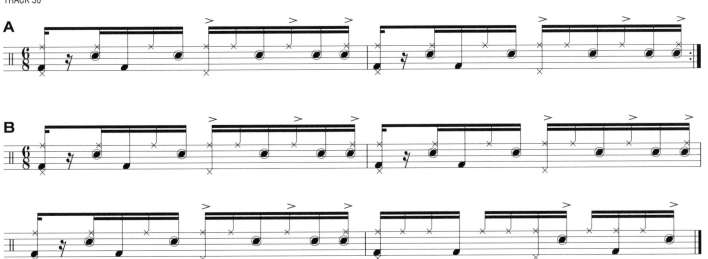

As you play different 6/8 grooves, try working in the Nanigo rhythm.

For more information on Nanigo and 6/8 grooves, check out *Afro-Cuban Coordination for Drumset* by Maria Martinez, *World Beat Rhythms Series: Africa* and *Cuba* by Ed Roscetti and Maria Martinez, and *Drummer's Guide to Odd Meters* by Ed Roscetti. All titles are published by Hal Leonard.

ODD METERS

Odd meters are those that are in odd-numbered time signatures (3/4, 5/8, 7/8, etc.), as opposed to those that are even-numbered time signatures (4/4, 2/4, 2/2, etc.). The rhythmic possibilities utilizing odd meters are endless. Studying and playing different grooves in odd times opens the mind to different rhythmic subdivisions that will increase your rhythmic vocabulary, thereby improving your ability to handle any odd-time situation, and even enhancing your 4/4 playing. The key is to learn to interpret groups of three eighth notes, within any style. You already know how to play and feel groups of two eighth notes from playing in 4/4 time. It may be the groups of three eighth notes that will be foreign to you at first. An odd meter such as 7/8 most often consists of two groups of two eighth notes and one group of three eighth notes. So, instead of counting "1-2-3-4-5-6-7" for 7/8 time, one method of counting would be "1-2-1-2-1-2-3" for a measure where the last three eighth notes are grouped together.

You may also encounter 7/8 meters where the group of three eighth notes begins the measure; you would count this "1-2-3-1-2-1-2." It all depends on the musical phrase and how the music is subdivided into rhythms.

By using this method it won't matter to you what time signature you're in. You will eventually feel the subdivided groupings of two and three eighth notes within the phrase and stylize it. Let's begin with the *Rhythmic Guide* concept (more on p. 96).

The Rhythmic Guide concept is a breakdown of rhythms that can be applied to any given rhythmic subdivision in any meter. These rhythmic drills will increase your rhythmic awareness and vocabulary. Use the Rhythmic Guide Examples A–M that follow these steps.

1) Start off playing Example D hand-to-hand to an eighth-note click. Count the sixteenth notes 1-e-an-da, 2-e-an-da, 1-2-3, 1-2-3.

2) Play Example B as an ostinato with your right or left foot while playing the other examples against it. Always alternate each example with Example D. For instance, play two bars of D into two bars of J, and then back to D and into M. Jump around the letters, i.e., D, J, D, C, D, M, D, L, etc.

3) Play Example D on the hi-hat while playing Example F on the bass drum. This produces a basic 7/8 samba feel. Since traditional samba is in cut time (2/2), to make the 7/8 samba rhythm feel more like it's in two, accent the downbeat of the second group of two, and the last dotted eighth note in the bar (see Example F).

RHYTHMIC GUIDE

Add some of your own rhythms to the 7/8 Rhythmic Guide and write your own guides using different 7/8 subdivisions.

The next example is a samba groove in 7/8. The seven is subdivided 1-2-1-2-1-2-3. Some of the rhythms used are taken from the 7/8 Rhythmic Guide.

The downbeat and the last dotted quarter note in the phrase are accented (as in the first and last notes of the cowbell part below). This produces the feeling of two in seven. To make **Track 51**, first the drumset part was played to a cowbell click of two quarter notes and a dotted quarter note. Next, a shaker, cowbell, 12" wooden djembe cajon, and a talking drum part were overdubbed. Only the two-bar basic groove is written out below, but **Track 51** takes things a bit further.

Work on developing the samba feel and other grooves in 7/8 time. Remember to go to the *Five Steps to Musicality* (p. 42) for the second concept. You should run all of your rhythms down through the five steps.

In Examples O–U below, repeat the same procedure that you used with the 7/8 guide. Use examples O and R as ostinatos in your feet. Play the other examples against them. Use Q as the basic rhythm, and jump around playing two-bar phrases.

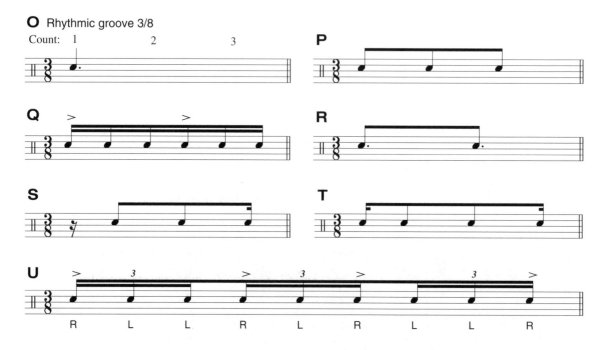

Example V is a 6/8 rock groove. On **Track 52**, there is a two-bar fill up front, and the rest is organized into eight-bar phrases. Try your hand at writing out (transcribing) the intro fills and the fills played during the turnarounds on this track. Also write some grooves and fills of your own in 6/8 time. For more information on this subject, see my book/CD *Drummer's Guide to Odd Meters* (Hal Leonard).

TRACK 52

OSTINATO

An *ostinato* is a phrase that happens over and over again. There are many examples of the use of ostinatos in this book. For one example, see *Samba* (p. 107) and listen to **Track 72**, where I play the samba bass drum phrase, and play over it with my hands. In this case, the ostinato is in the bass drum. Check out the theme from *Mission: Impossible*, which is in 5/4 time. The ostinato is in the brass part in that composition.

The next examples demonstrate a basic ostinato in the bass drum. Examples A and B show the bass drum only, as it occurs in two slightly different forms. Examples C and D show other parts added to the ostinato. **Track 53** uses these bass drum ostinatos in a groove which begins with a part being played on the rim of the snare drum with the right hand, while the left hand plays cross stick. All four examples demonstrate the basic concepts used on **Track 53**.

TRACK 53

Work on writing and playing some of your own grooves with ostinato bass drum phrases.

OVER AND THROUGH THE BAR LINE

To be able to groove in the style you wish to play, you need to play effortlessly over and through the bar line within a phrase of any length. Before you can do this, you must be able to play your basic groove in the given style. **Track 54** plays a samba feel in two (cut time, 2/2), with Blasticks. The phrasing is made up of four bars of time and then four bars of a solo fill. The fill is played over the bar line of the last measure, extending to beat 2 of the first bar that returns to time playing. As the four-bar phrases progress, more is played (on the CD), but the basic vibe of the phrasing is the same. The first sixteen bars are included in the next example. Remember that your whole body needs to feel two to play in two. For more, see *Samba* (p. 107).

TRACK 54

You should also work on playing the upbeats of the sixteenth notes to get you through the bar line. For more information on this subject, check out my book/CDs *Drummer's Guide to Odd Meters* and *World Beat Rhythms Series: Brazil*, *Africa*, and *Cuba* (Hal Leonard).

OVERDUB

Overdubbing involves adding and recording a new part to a pre-existing track.

The drumset as an overdub instrument

Step back and look at a five-piece drum set. What do you see? A bass drum, three tom-toms, snare drum, hi-hat, ride cymbal, and two crashes. Start off by moving all the drums, cymbals, and hi-hat away from the bass drum. You are now left with the bass drum. Sit behind the bass drum, put on a song that you like to play along with (in 4/4 time), and just play quarter notes on the bass drum all the way through the song. When you want to break it down, play half notes or whole notes. Move your arms as if you're playing hi-hat and snare to help you get in the groove. Feel free to move and dance on the pedal. Find your dance. Every drummer has his/her dance. Your dance is how your body moves when you are moving your time-feel in the groove.

When you finish working on the bass drum, add the snare drum and repeat the process. This time, remember to play the snare drum only (no bass drum), then repeat the process with the hi-hat, ride cymbal, crash cymbal, and tom-toms. This will help you think of each piece of the drumset individually. Why do we need to do this? Today's drum tracks are sometimes a combination of programmed beats (using samples), loops, and real-time overdubs (i.e., with real instruments). For example, you might have to overdub tom fills, a real hi-hat, or real ride cymbal to a drum loop. One time I had to do a snare drum overdub to a programmed loop using brushes. I have also overdubbed bass drum only, played tom fills, or played just hi-hat in the studio. The possibilities are endless. You can make all kinds of sounds with a basic five-piece drumset.

The floor tom can be used as a *surdo* (Brazilian drum), as the heartbeat of the groove. Your smaller toms can be depressed by pushing down on the heads with your thumb while playing. This will give you the sound of a talking drum. You can hit the rims or the side of your floor tom for a sharp sounding attack. Also try scraping your cymbals with the metal back of one of your brushes. Experiment with different sounds and think of each piece of the kit as a separate instrument that can be used as an overdub instrument.

 Track 55 is a groove featuring a loop of the bass drum and snare groove. All the cymbals were overdubbed later. Check it out and spend some time working on overdubbing on the drumset.

TRACK 55

PRACTICE

To set up a fulfilling practice routine, make a category list of what you want to work on, and create a practice room that is comfortable, well-ventilated, and feels good to be in. See the list below for an example.

Category List

- Reading
- Rudiments
- Technique
- Styles (rock, hip-hop, jazz, Latin)
- Play-along CDs
- Click (playing with a click, loops, and sequences)
- Internal clock

Work on each category for half an hour. The key is to focus on what you are doing and you will have a productive practice session. Remember that practicing can sometimes involve just playing, unless you are working on a specific technique. Always play in phrases and over a form.

You can practice something for ten minutes and accomplish a lot if you're really focused. You can also practice for six hours, get nothing done, and be all over the place if you are unfocused.

When you are away from the drums, keep your ears open and do a lot of listening. This is also a form of practicing. Remember, it's not always how long you practice, but how well!

PLAY-ALONG

A "play-along" is a recording that has an instrumental part missing from the mix so that the musician can play that missing part along with the recording as if part of the band. A drum play-along CD would include the band minus the drums.

Spend time playing and practicing to a click, with loops, sequenced tracks, and working on your internal clock. It's a good idea to have tracks to play along with at the end of your practice routine. Look for book/CD packages that have good songs to perform with and a variety of tempos in the desired style. This interaction will help you to practice playing down the middle of the track.

Track 56 is a funk style play-along track recorded with a full band, minus drumset. Developing a strong and consistent backbeat is very important when you are playing funk grooves. Listen to the track and concentrate on feeling the downbeats. Examples A–F can be played along with the Introduction and A Section of **Track 56**. The forward motion in the time-feel of this groove comes from quarter notes. Accenting the quarter note will give a strong downbeat feeling in the lope of the hi-hat and ride cymbal. The unaccented snare notes should be played softly (i.e., as *ghost notes*), and the accented snare notes should be played as backbeats. The tempo of the chart is ♩ = 96 bpm.

TRACK 56

A Grooves for the Intro and A Section

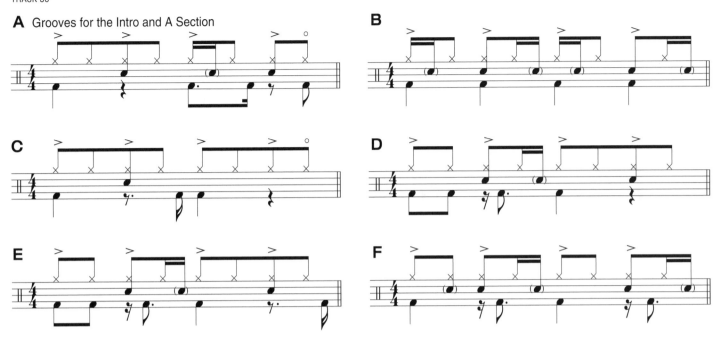

B

C

D

E

F

The following two-bar grooves work with Section B of the chart. These grooves are more syncopated than the A Section grooves. You may notice that G and H are very similar to each other, but pay close attention to the accents.

G Grooves for the B Section
(Downbeats in the hi-hat)

H (Upbeats in the hi-hat)

Next are a few two-beat fills that you can use with the chart. Make sure your fills come from the groove of your time-feel.

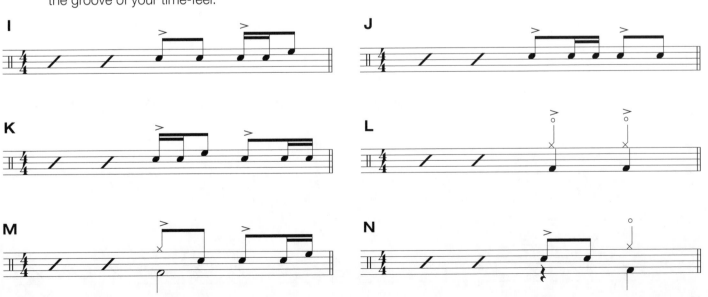

I

J

K

L

M

N

Before we play the chart, let's check out the ensemble figure that appears in the 2nd ending of Section A. The rhythm has been subdivided for you using sixteenth notes so you can easily see the syncopation.

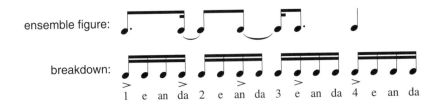

Now it's time to play with the chart for **Track 56**. Use the grooves, fills, and phrases from Examples A–M to play the chart. Then play your own grooves and fills, and have fun with it.

CHART NOTES

Intro	8 bars
A1	8 bars
A2	8 bars
B1	16 bars

TRACK 56

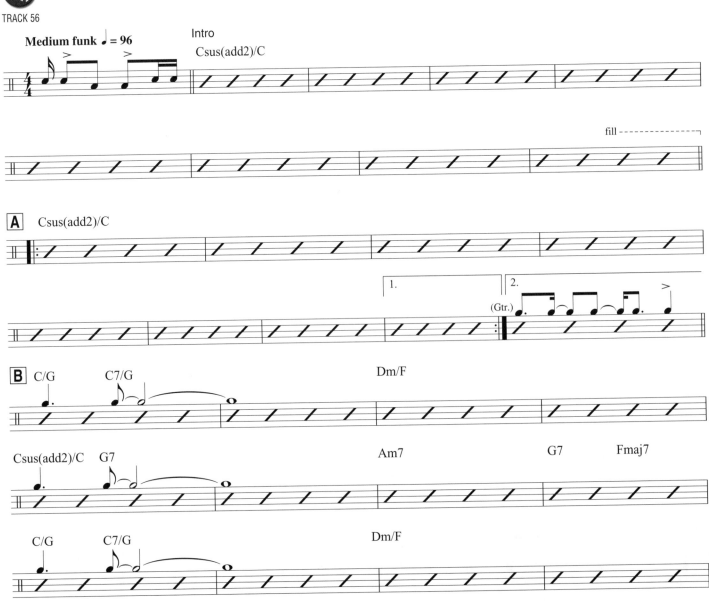

86

PROGRAMMING

Back in the '80s, drum programming was done with drum machines. Examples include the Linn Drum, the Roland TR-808, the Roland R-8, and the Yamaha RX-7. Today, most drummers who program beats use a computer. It is the norm that digital sampling libraries, drum and percussion loop libraries, or custom libraries are software-based and tied into Logic, Pro Tools, or Digital Performer, or some other recording/sequencing software. Sounds are triggered from electronic pads (i.e., pad to MIDI converters) or a keyboard controller.

Track 57 is a hip-hop groove that was programmed into Logic with an M-Audio 88 weighted-key keyboard controller. The sounds were samples from my EX-24 sampler in Logic. Remember that when you are programming beats, it doesn't matter what program or software you're using. Find a program that works for you and make your beats feel like an extension of your own playing by using different increments of swing and *quantization* (time correction to nearest beat chosen). You can always program in real time and then experiment with different percentages and combinations of quantizing.

TRACK 57

Have fun programming your own beats and percussion loops to which you'll be playing along.

PRO TOOLS

Pro Tools is a digital audio workstation that integrates hardware and software. It is widely used by professionals in music production, post production, and TV and film scoring.

As one of the first programs to provide CD-quality (16 bit, 44.1 kHz) multitrack digital audio editing on a personal computer, Pro Tools grew quickly in the sound recording field, becoming popular because of its streamlined interface for non-linear, non-destructive editing. This appealed to producers, composers, and musicians who switched to computer-based digital audio production from analog. In 2004, Digidesign received a technical Academy Award of Merit for the development of Pro Tools.

As a drummer on a session, making a pass (a beginning-to-end take) is fast becoming a thing of the past. *Grid mode* (audio regions and MIDI notes that are moved or inserted into a user-defined time grid that can be set to quarter notes, eighth notes, etc.) and "cut and paste" are the norm for producers in pop music today. Usually you will play the song down a couple of times, then it is edited and loops are made from your original performance. You must be able to play down the middle of the time-feel. This will help you when the editors are working in grid mode. Note: The CD on this project was recorded on Pro Tools LE and HD systems.

PUNK

Punk is an aggressive form of politically-driven rock. It originally gained momentum as part of a profoundly politicized movement in London, serving as a beacon of teenage angst and rebellion. The style was set into motion by Sex Pistols manager Malcolm McLaren, and developed in the late 1970s in the United Kingdom, the United States, and Australia. Groups like the Sex Pistols, The Ramones, and The Clash were recognized as the guiding force of this new musical movement. With bare-bones instrumentation, simple chord structures, a disdain for polished performances, and confrontational lyrics, these bands distanced themselves from mainstream 1970s rock, and brought a new energy and reckless abandon to the forefront of popular music. An international style emerged from the music as the punk subculture gained expression through fetishist clothing, a climate of anti-establishment themes, and the alienation and lowered expectations of 1970s youth.

Recommended Listening

- The Ramones, *Ramones* (1976)
- The Saints, *I'm Stranded* (Aust. 1976; U.S. 1977)
- The Sex Pistols, *Never Mind the Bollocks, Here's the Sex Pistols* (1977)
- The Clash, *The Clash* (U.K. 1977; U.S. 1979)
- The Damned, *Damned Damned Damned* (1977)
- Wire, *Pink Flag* (1977)

 Track 58 demonstrates three possible punk grooves, the first of which (Example A) features an insistent crash/ride punctuated by accents on the snare in the intro.

TRACK 58

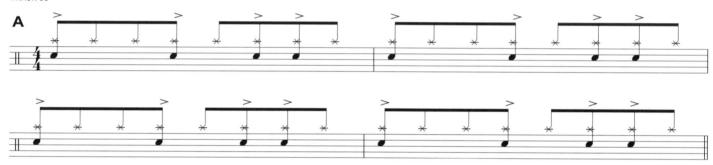

The second groove (Example B) is a tom-tom groove with snare backbeat.

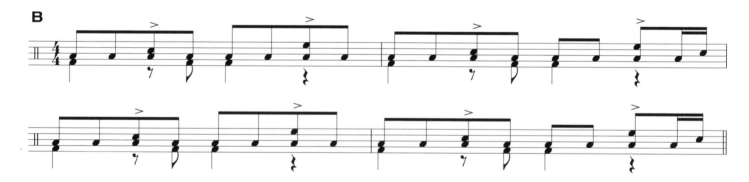

The third groove (Example C) has that "reckless abandon riding-on-the-crash" vibe.

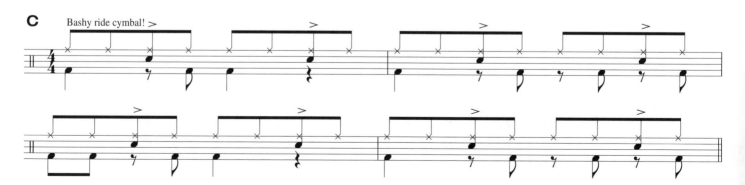

In punk, the style on the drumset has a looser, sloppier vibe to it, so make sure to play these grooves with the right attitude.

PEDALS (BASS DRUM AND HI-HAT)

When choosing a bass drum pedal and hi-hat stand you should look for pedals and stands that are comfortable to play, easy to adjust, and durable. Some drummers have elaborate pedal setups, triggering a multitude of drums, hi-hat stands, effects, and electronics. Terry Bozzio uses six bass drum pedals and five hi-hats with custom linkage in his setup.

I like to keep it simple: one bass drum pedal and one hi-hat stand. Hey, whatever combination works for you is what you should use. On the accompanying CD, I played both a DW chain bass drum pedal and a DW bass drum pedal with a strap. The strap pedal is still one of my favorites.

When you have to sit in behind a strange kit and the pedal feels like an alien being, play quarter notes on the bass drum and groove. Don't sweat it. Remember to keep all your pedals clean and well lubricated. DW-40 works well for springs and sprockets.

QUARTER-NOTE GROOVES

The quarter-note (four-on-the-floor) groove is one of the strongest bass drum phrases in 4/4 time. To this day, you can play this phrase on the bottom of almost any style of music.

A

The old disco and R&B grooves used big four-on-the-floor grooves. So did Stewart Copeland in many Police songs. Four-on-the-floor is big when playing shuffles, as well as rock, funk, hip-hop, and certain Latin grooves.

The next example is a groove in the style of the Police. This is four-on-the-floor, with a reggae ska feel on the top. The basic groove is notated in Example B, though **Track 59** goes a bit further.

TRACK 59

B

Example C is a rock groove with toms on the backbeat and half notes on the bass drum. The splashy hi-hat and the djembe cajon parts were overdubbed. You can break down to half notes on the bass drum from a four-on-the-floor groove to create more space in the bottom of the groove.

TRACK 60

C

Work on some four-on-the-floor grooves of your own in different styles. Remember, when in doubt, quarter-note bass drum rules.

READING

I get these questions a lot when I'm conducting clinics: "How important is it to read if you are a drummer?" "How often do you have to read?"

It's extremely important to be able to read snare drum music and to be able to follow and interpret charts. Reading is essential on all instruments. The more quickly you relate to the chart, the more musical you can be. In many instances you will have to read. Using your ears is a good thing, but it's not enough. You need to be able to read *and* use your ears. Read the chart and then use your ears to get your head out of the chart while listening to the band so you can groove and play what's best for the song.

Joe Porcaro told me years ago that learning how to read was all about repetition. You read music a little bit every day and before you know it, new snare drum pieces and drum charts are easier to read. The figures and rhythms start to look more familiar over a period of time. Once you can read and keep your place, it's all about the interpretation of the chart in the given style, as well as the groove and being supportive of the melody.

The following example is a reading exercise that will help you with the different note values and the counting of rhythms. Play each bar twice and then move on to the next bar. Count the rhythms out loud and use alternate sticking (R-L-R-L). Play to a click at different tempos.

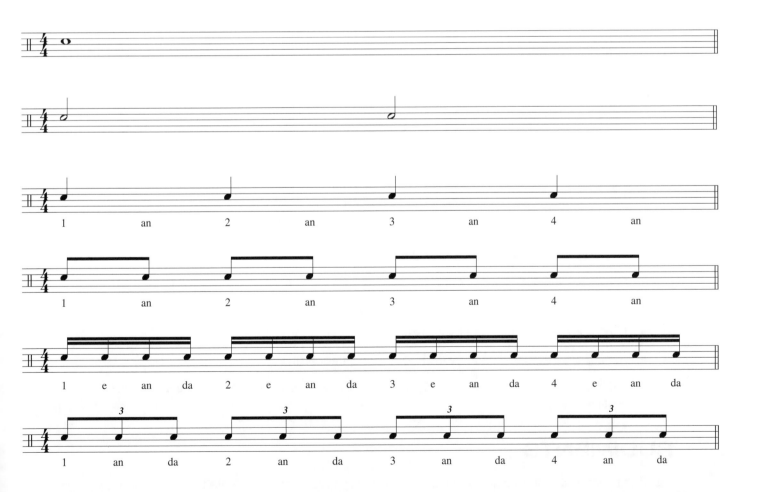

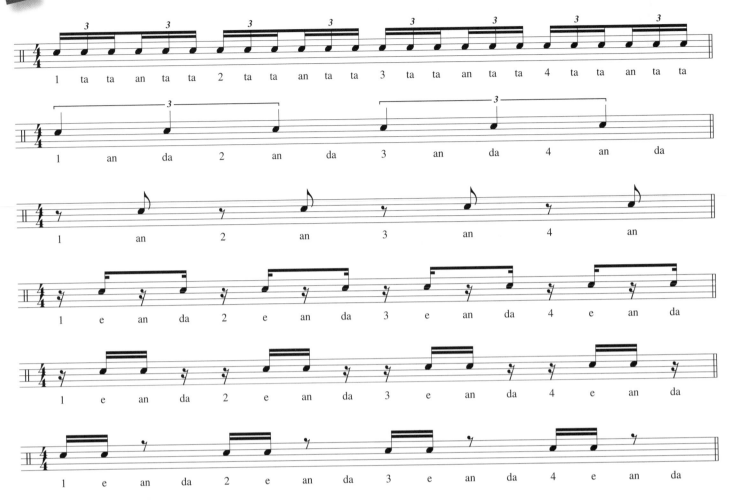

Becoming a better sight-reader (*sight-reading*: reading a chart for the first time having never seen nor practiced it before; a good sight reader can see a chart for the first time and play it down) again comes down to repetition and experience. Sight-reading a chart is like telling a story for the first time—you need to make your point—get in and get out.

Remember to read a little bit every day. It's a good idea to work on your reading with a teacher. It's all about the repetition.

The following publications are good sources for snare drum, drumset, and chart reading:

- *Drummer's Guide to Odd Meters* by Ed Roscetti (Hal Leonard)
- *Rudimental Warm-ups* by Maria Martinez (Hal Leonard)
- *Joe Porcaro's Drumset Method* by Joe Porcaro (JoPo Music)
- *Progressive Steps to Syncopation for the Modern Drummer* by Ted Reed (Alfred)
- *Blues Drumming* by Ed Roscetti (Hal Leonard)
- *Funk & Hip-Hop Drumming* by Ed Roscetti (Hal Leonard)
- *Rock Drumming Workbook* by Ed Roscetti (Hal Leonard)
- *World Beat Rhythms Series: Brazil, Africa,* and *Cuba* by Ed Roscetti and Maria Martinez (Hal Leonard)

RUDIMENTS

Rudiments are to the drummer what scales are to the pianist. They coordinate the hands and work the muscles. Their application to the drumset is endless.

Example A is a rudiment called the paradiddle-diddle. On **Track 61**, it is played on the snare drum. You should start off playing all of the rudiments on the snare drum and then work on moving them over to the drumset.

Example B takes the paradiddle-diddle and plays it over a jazz swing feel. This version is written in eighth-note triplets. The phrasing is four bars of time into four bars of the paradiddle-diddle. This eight-bar phrase happens three times with the orchestration of the paradiddle-diddle on the drumset changing each time.

After you learn the paradiddle-diddle on the snare and learn the orchestrations on the drumset, experiment with a few ideas of your own using the paradiddle-diddle rudiment.

Examples C–F give a few more rudiments for you to learn. It is highly recommended that you study all the rudiments with a teacher. Learning these will take your playing to a higher level. For more information on the rudiments and how to apply them to the drumset, check out *Joe Porcaro's Drumset Method* by Joe Porcaro (JoPo Music) and *Rudimental Warm-ups* by Maria Martinez (Hal Leonard).

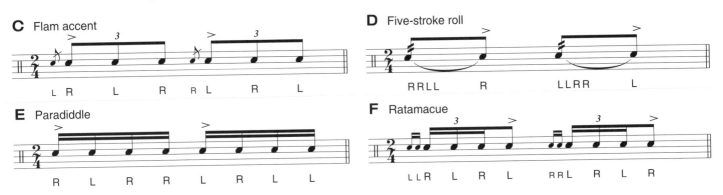

C Flam accent

L R   L   R   R L   R   L

D Five-stroke roll

R R L L   R   L L R R   L

E Paradiddle

R   L   R   R   L   R   L   L

F Ratamacue

L L R   L   R   L   R R L   R   L   R

RIDE CYMBAL

The ride cymbal and the hi-hat are the center for timekeeping on the drumset. The ride is struck with brushes or sticks to create a reverberating, shimmering sound. It is often played in rhythmic phrases to dictate the pulse or time of a composition, which is how the name "ride" was adopted. Its sound quality makes it a favorite above other cymbals, as it can be struck repeatedly without overpowering or drawing attention away from other components of the song.

Standard ride diameters range from 18" to 24", with 20" to 22" being the most common. There are also different thicknesses to choose from, depending on the musical style being played. For example, a jazz combo may require a thin, dark, washy sound, whereas larger, thicker cymbals may be needed for higher-volume situations, as in a rock performance. Stick attack and shape of the bead of the stick will change the sound as well.

TRACK 63

Track 63 uses a 20" Paiste Light Traditional ride, played in a jazz swing feel. Listen to the different sounds of the ride cymbal.

When you pick out a ride cymbal, make sure that you play it with the rest of your cymbals on your drumset so you can hear how it blends with your other cymbals. Always use the sticks that you will be playing within the style. Have someone else play the ride while you step back and listen. This way you can hear how the sound blends with the drumset and your other cymbals in the room.

The following is a list of rides used on the accompanying CD:

20" Traditional Light Ride (Paiste)

20" Traditional Medium Heavy Ride (Paiste)

20" Traditional Extra Light Crash/Ride (Paiste)

20" Giant Beat Crash (used as a ride) (Paiste)

22" Dark Energy Mark 1 Ride (Paiste)

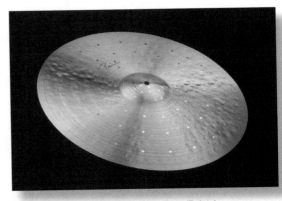
20" Traditional Light Ride (Paiste)

20" Traditional Medium Heavy Ride (Paiste)

20" Giant Beat Crash (used as a ride) (Paiste)

22" Dark Energy Mark 1 Ride (Paiste)

REPETITION

Saturating yourself in the style that you are trying to learn or improve on takes time, consistency, and repetition. Working on a groove, fill, or ensemble figure over and over again until you own it in the style is a must. Repetition is the answer. Revisit and repeat what you think you know again and again until it is part of your vocabulary. Rhythmic figures and longer phrases will become easier to read by using repetition when you practice. You will see many of the same rhythms that you have seen in the past, mixed up in different phrases. Repetition is key!

ROAD

Being on the road can be challenging at times, what with long hours in between gigs, delays at airports, and/or long bus rides. Taking care of yourself when you're on tour is a must to stay healthy and fit for playing the show. You have your sound check before the show and the show might be only ninety minutes long. How you spend the rest of your time will have a bearing on how you sound the next night. Below are a few tips to keep you road-worthy:

- Get the rest you need.
- Don't stay up all night and party.
- Get some exercise.
- Stretch.
- Eat right.
- Drink a lot of water.
- Take vitamins.
- Bring a practice pad with you.
- Don't stay in the hotel all the time. Get out and breathe some air.

- If you're in a cool place and have the time, check out the city you're visiting.
- Read.
- Stay in touch with your loved ones back home.
- Have a good attitude when you're with your co-workers.
- Have your paycheck directly deposited into your bank account.
- Ask for your weekly per diem in cash, if possible. This way you can live off your per diem and save your paycheck.

There will always be obstacles to overcome on the road, even in the best situations. Have a good time and learn to hang. Remember that you're out there to make music, not to create drama.

RHYTHMIC GUIDE

A *Rhythmic Guide* is a breakdown of rhythms that can be applied to any given rhythmic subdivision in any meter. These rhythmic drills will increase your rhythmic awareness and vocabulary.

This tip is one of two unique concepts. After you have checked out this *Rhythmic Guide* concept, go to *Five Steps to Musicality* (p. 42). Listen to **Track 64** while looking at Examples A–O. Each example is played twice so you can hear the rhythms clearly. After you listen, follow the directions below.

 RHYTHMIC GUIDE

see *Five Steps to Musicality* (p. 42)

TRACK 64

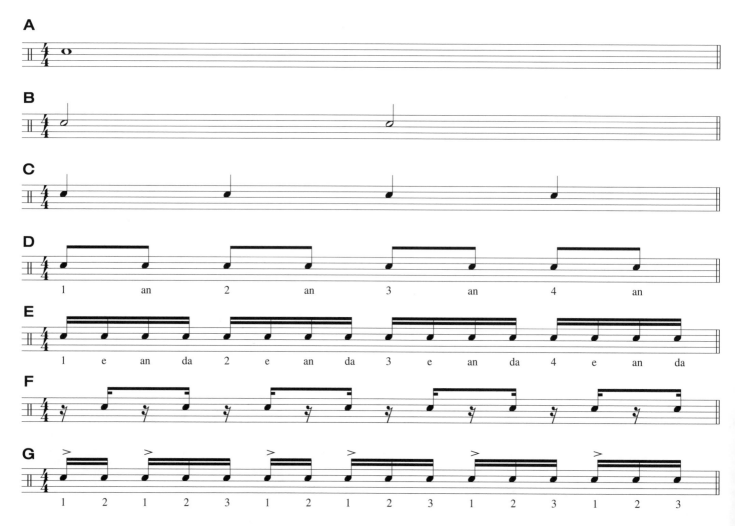

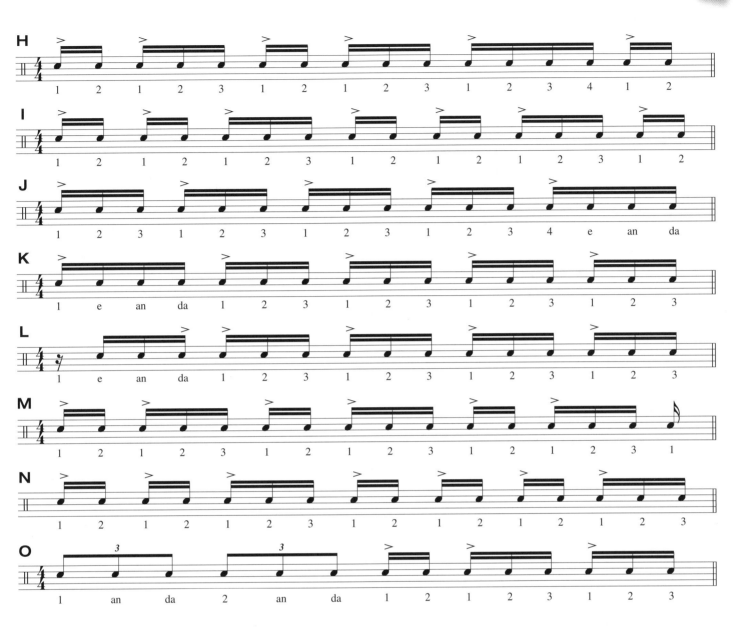

Start by playing these rhythms away from the drumset. Use your hands on your lap, a hand drum, or play them on a table top, tapping your foot to a quarter-note pulse. Most of the sixteenth notes are subdivided into groups of ones, twos, and threes. Play each measure twice and then proceed to the next measure. After you are comfortable with all the rhythms, move to the drumset and repeat the same procedure on the snare drum playing A, B, or C as the bass drum ostinato. Next, randomly jump around the *Rhythmic Guide*, creating your own two-, four-, or eight-bar phrases. For example, use letter E as the basic rhythm and jump to a new rhythm, (i.e., F, upbeats), each time returning to E, and then moving into a new rhythm. This approach will help you internalize the rhythms, both at and away from the drumset.

Start making grooves from the rhythms and sing bass ostinatos against your grooves while playing. For more on this, see *Five Steps to Musicality* (p. 42).

Another approach is to play a sixteenth-note groove with an egg shaker in one hand, and the sixteenth-note upbeats with the other hand, against a bass drum ostinato, while singing the other rhythms out loud. After you have mastered this routine at different tempos, write your own Rhythmic Guides in any meter and create more complex bass drum ostinatos to play against. Work on this system and your rhythmic vocabulary will grow. Then you can move on to the second concept (*Five Steps to Musicality*) with all your new rhythms.

REGGAE

Reggae is a modern popular music and dance style of Jamaica. The rhythmic style originated in the mid-1960s, becoming a worldwide trend in the 1970s. Reggae continues to dominate the Jamaican digital pop music of the present day.

This rhythmic style has a strong upbeat accent on the offbeats that is usually played on a lead rhythm guitar in short ostinato phrases. This is called the *skank*. Another Jamaican rhythm called *ska* is usually played faster than reggae and implies a shuffle feel similar to classic rhythm and blues. Other than the occasional alternative treatment by some artists (i.e., Sting), the reggae style is usually played in 4/4 time because the rhythm does not lend itself to other time signatures such as 3/4 or odd times. The drummer for the Police, Stewart Copeland, used many reggae and ska rhythms in his grooves. He would play four-on-the-floor (with the bass drum) along with syncopated reggae and ska rhythms in his hands on top.

Bob Marley led the reggae movement in the 1970s with his group The Wailers. Most reggae songs are made up of a simple, repetitive chord progression, adding to the hypnotic effect of this style.

In the next example, the strong accent of the groove is on beat 3 of each bar, played on the bass drum and side stick. The hi-hat has an upbeat syncopated feel. The example is also organized in eight-bar phrases. The first eight bars are included below, but **Track 65** goes further.

TRACK 65

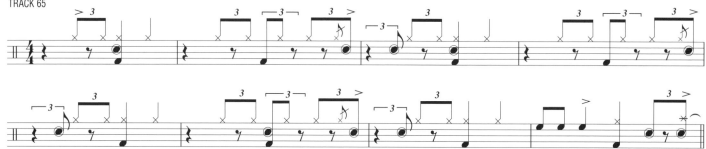

ROCK

Rock is a musical genre comprised of a combination of black R&B and white country music that arose in the United States in the mid-1950s, and has since become the dominant form of pop music worldwide.

In the beginning years of rock 'n' roll, African American artists such as Chuck Berry, Little Richard, Bo Diddley, and Fats Domino played their original material predominantly to African American crowds. As rock gained in popularity and became more commercially viable, white artists with major labels including Elvis Presley, Bill Haley & His Comets, Buddy Holly, Jerry Lee Lewis, and Johnny Cash covered their music, bringing it across the lines in racially divided dancehalls by touring throughout the U.S. and Britain. Cultural intermingling slowly resulted from the breaking down of racial boundaries in radio, recordings, and television.

There is much debate over what the first true rock 'n' roll song is. But, in 1953, Bill Haley & His Comets was the first rock 'n' roll band to be listed on the *Billboard* charts with their song "Crazy Man Crazy," and again in 1955 with their number-one hit "Rock Around the Clock."

Drummer Ringo Starr arrived in the U.S. in 1963 with the Beatles to kick off the British Invasion with their appearance on the Ed Sullivan Show. The wild adulation they received became known as Beatlemania. Even though I was only four years old when I saw the Beatles on that show, I still remember watching Ringo behind that Ludwig kit. The U.S.

would never be the same after that performance—the Beatles changed music forever that evening. Groups like the Rolling Stones (with drummer Charlie Watts), The Yardbirds, and The Animals were soon to follow.

The first Woodstock concert in 1969 was the largest outdoor rock concert at that time in history. Around 500,000 people gathered on farmland in upstate New York to experience three days of fun, art, and music. Just a few of the many bands that performed were Jimi Hendrix; The Who; Santana; Joe Cocker; and Crosby, Stills & Nash.

The 1970s saw the rise of singer-songwriters such as Joni Mitchell, Paul Simon, Neil Young, Elton John, David Bowie, and Bruce Springsteen, and the style spawned other forms of rock such as jazz-rock, heavy metal, punk, grunge, and speed metal. Today, rock continues to have a huge global impact.

Examples A–H feature an up-tempo quarter-note rock feel. Practice these two-bar grooves after you listen to the full band on **Track 66**. Then write some rock grooves of your own.

TRACK 66

Notable Rock Drummers

- John Bonham (Led Zeppelin)
- Jeff Porcaro (Toto)
- Keith Moon (The Who)
- Ian Paice (Deep Purple)
- Danny Carey (Tool)

- Ringo Starr (The Beatles)
- Neil Peart (Rush)
- Stewart Copeland (Police)
- Alex Van Halen (Van Halen)
- Russ Kunkel (Jackson Browne, James Taylor)

REST

A rest is a notational symbol that indicates silence. Rest points in music create space. If everyone in the rhythm section played on every beat, the groove would not breath and there would be no space. When you're creating a groove for a song, always leave space for the other instruments.

Rest points also work well in creating longer phrases. Example A below is a rhythmic phrase using two rest points in the second bar to help create the four-bar phrase.

The following are a few more rhythmic phrases utilizing rest points. Example B is in 7/8 time and Example C is in 6/8. Write and experiment with rest points on your own and you will see how your phrasing will open up.

RHYTHM SECTION

The rhythm section is the portion of the band that creates the groove (i.e., drums, bass, rhythm guitar, and keyboards). The instrumentation of the rhythm section will vary depending on the style of music. But in any case, the drummer is the leader of the rhythm section, even if he/she is not technically the leader of the whole band (the pied piper, so to speak). As the leader, you want to instill confidence in everyone so they can lean on and follow you. A drummer who does not take control of the time-feel will be a follower, pushed and pulled in every direction but their own. Commit to your groove and your time-feel, and people will follow you. This does not mean that you shouldn't take direction from the leader or conductor. But, once you're groovin', you must put it where you think it should be with confidence and authority.

TRACK 67

Track 67 plays a quarter-note bass drum with a big rock half-time feel, with the backbeat and cymbal crash on beat 3. Some tom fills are included in between the backbeats. Try to transcribe the groove, then learn it and write some grooves of your own. And remember, the drummer is the pied piper of the rhythm section!

SNARE DRUM

The snare is a round cylindrical drum. It is usually crafted from different types of wood (maple or birch) or metal, and has animal skin (old school) or plastic heads (easier to tune) stretched over the top and bottom parts of the drum. Located at the center of the drumset, it is the key to this entire set of instruments. By changing the size or sound of your snare drum, you can change the vibe of your entire kit.

The *snares* (eight or more wires on the resonant bottom head) give the drum its crisp resonance when the lower head vibrates against them. A snare drum should breathe, and the feel should be responsive. If the snares aren't right, it can alter the way you hit the drum, which can affect your technique and change your overall sound on the drumset. Your muscular system will react to the sound and feel of your snare drum.

Snare drums come in many different sizes as well. The size affects the way the drum sounds. Snare drums that are shallow in size will give a higher "cracking" sound, while the larger drums will give a deeper, heavier, and thicker tone. The same is true of drums with a smaller diameter. Many drummers choose to include more than one snare drum in their setup to create a broader dynamic range.

Track 68 features a rudimental march cadence on a 14" bronze snare drum (Pacific). Listen to the dynamic range of the drum.

TRACK 68

When you're picking out a snare drum, make sure you keep in mind the style of music that you will be playing. Experiment with different snare drums to get the sound you're looking for. The following is a list of snare drums used on the accompanying CD.

5 ½" x 14" bronze snare (Pacific)

5 ½" x 14" wooden snare (Pacific)

5 ½" x 15" wooden snare w/wooden hoops (Pacific)

5 ½" x 14" metal-edge snare (DW)

10" popcorn snare, wooden (Pacific)

3 ½" x 14" piccolo snare, wooden (Pacific)

5 ½" x 14" Vintage Black Beauty metal snare (Ludwig)

5 ½" X 14" bronze snare (Pacific)

5 ½" X 14" wooden snare (Pacific)

3 ½" X 14" piccolo snare, wooden (Pacific)

5 ½" X 14" metal-edge snare (DW)

10" popcorn snare, wooden (Pacific)

SNARE WIRES

Snare wires are strings of metal, gut, nylon, or wire-covered silk (usually eight or more in number) that are stretched across the bottom resonant head of a snare drum. The tension of the snare wires is regulated by the use of an on/off screw mechanism. If it is turned off, the snare drum will have a high-pitched tom sound. If it is turned on and adjusted correctly, a crisp brilliant tone will be created.

Snare wires give the drum its crisp resonance when the lower head vibrates against them. Drum dimensions, quality of craftsmanship, materials, the number of lugs used for tuning, and the snare wires themselves are among the determinants of a snare sound. The wires give the drum its characteristic resonance and timbre. When the upper drumhead is hit, that movement is communicated to the lower head, which in turn vibrates against the wires.

In the selection of snares, it's important to take into consideration both the design of your drum and the type of sound you are looking to create with it. Often overlooked is the importance of the snare bed, which creates a bow in the center of the bottom head. This bow allows a greater amount of contact between the drumhead and the snare wires themselves. See the snare option chart below.

PURESOUND SNARE WIRE OPTIONS AND PERFORMANCE CHART

Performance Category	Custom	Equalizer	Varitone	221
strands	12, 16, 20, 24	16, 20, 24	16	8
gauge	standard	standard	light, medium, heavy	standard
placement	center	off-set	center	center
coils	standard	standard	standard	2-to-1
tone	mid-range	mid-range	dark, mid, bright	dark
decay	mid-range	dry	mid-range	dry
spread	variable	variable	mid-range	maximum
articulation	variable	variable	mid-range	mid-range
sensitivity	mid-range	mid-range	variable	moderate
balance	variable	variable	mid-range	active

Snare Wire Performance Terms: *Articulation* – the clarity of each stroke. *Balance* – the prominence of the snare sound in relation to the drum sound. *Coils* – the spacing of the spirals in the wire. *Decay* – the duration of the sound. *Gauge* – the weight or thickness of the wire. *Placement* – the position of the strands on the drumhead. *Sensitivity* - the responsiveness of the wires. *Spread* – the thickness and texture of the overall snare sound. *Strands* – the individual wires in a set. *Tone* – the timbral quality of sound; i.e. bright, dark, etc. *Variable* – the performance characteristic can be altered by the specific model selected.

Experiment with different snare wires on your snare drums to attain the sound that you are looking for, appropriate for the style you are playing.

STICKS

Sticks constitute an important part of the drummer's equipment. Usually the *tip* of a drumstick is used to strike a drum. There are many types of tips (or *beads*) manufactured, including those of a round, oval barrel, or diamond shape (usually made of wood or nylon). Sizes also vary depending on the desired usage and sound. By the late 1950s, nylon tips were introduced. Later, additional synthetic tips were developed. The long center portion of the stick is referred to as the *shaft*, and the opposite larger rounded end is called the *butt*. Try using different areas of the stick to get varied sounds from your drums and cymbals. Drummers customarily hold the stick with its balance point just beyond the hand.

Often used in pairs (one in each hand), specialty sticks produce different types of sounds depending on the attack and materials used to make them. For some examples, see *Brushes and Specialty Sticks* (p. 10).

Find sticks that suit your technique and the style of music you're playing. Don't try to play jazz with large top-heavy sticks, and don't try to play rock with light thin sticks. It's a good idea to roll drumsticks on a flat surface to check for straightness before purchasing them.

Experiment with different stick combinations. I like to choose from an assortment of sticks to give me the sound that I'm looking for. Finding the right stick combination for the music is how I go about it. The following is a list of sticks used on the accompanying CD:

- Jeff Porcaro Model (Regal Tip)
- Groovers (Regal Tip)
- Bob Gadson Maple (Regal Tip)
- Memo Acevedo Revolution, timbale/percussion (Regal Tip)
- Blastick (Regal Tip)
- TyPhoons (Regal Tip)
- Saul Goodman 7 mallets (Regal Tip)
- Saul Goodman 8 mallets (Regal Tip)
- Jeff Hamilton wire brushes (Regal Tip)

Blastick (Regal Tip)

Jeff Hamilton wire brushes (Regal Tip)

Jeff Porcaro Model (Regal Tip)

Saul Goodman 8 mallets (Regal Tip)

SPEED

Let's keep this simple. Most students I encounter want to build more speed behind the drumset, but actually, in my opinion, it's harder to play slower than faster. Try playing a pop ballad at ♩ = 50–55 bpm; *then* we can talk about speed.

To increase speed, choose what you want to work on—a rudiment, roll, groove, or fill. Let's say it's a groove. Play the groove at a tempo with which you are comfortable. Write down the tempo—for example, ♩ = 120. Every two or three days, increase the tempo by one bpm and play your groove. If you do this every two days, in one month you should be playing your groove at 135 bpm. That is an increase of 15 bpm in one month. If you need to take longer in between each raising of the tempo, do it. Take your time and you will increase your speed gradually without hurting yourself. (If you want to work on slower tempos, do the opposite.)

Remember, playing faster is only good if you sound believable groovin' at that tempo. If you need to learn a song and you're having a hard time playing the groove at the tempo of the CD, slow it down. Use the above practice technique, and in a few weeks you might be burning at your desired tempo.

STUDIO TIPS

The following is a list of studio recording tips based on over thirty years of experience on the job:

- Have your own sound.

- Make sure your equipment sounds great.

- Be on time.

- Be able to read a chart and make music out of it (i.e., keep your place).

- Use your ears as well as your eyes at all times.

- Lock in with the bass.

- Have a good attitude. Remember, you're there to serve the music and the client.

- Play for the music. Remember, the melody rules the show.

- Have a full bag of tricks (i.e., numerous ideas that can work).

- Commit to the part and to the groove.

- Be able to play with the click (down the middle, a little ahead, or a little behind).

- Be able to groove with loops and sequenced tracks (find a place within the groove).

- Learn about the business and know the recording pay scales for what you're doing. Join your professional musicians union.

- Learn what to ask for in your headphone mix (cue mix) so that you can relax and play.

- Put down an egg shaker pass to the click so you can groove with your own time-feel and turn the click down in your headphones.

- Don't overtune your drums. Find the sweet spot and let it be. If you need a different sound, put up a different drum or cymbal.

- Recommend someone else if you feel you're not right for the job or if you're too busy working on something else.

- Be a team player and be helpful.

- Learn to make a beginning-to-end, one-pass take (even though they're working in grid mode in Pro Tools and they're going to cut and paste you to death).

- Remember, it's music, not brain surgery. Have fun and groove!

SEQUENCED GROOVES

Sequenced grooves are beats that are programmed using a sequencer. **Track 69** features a programmed groove that was sequenced in Logic. It's a two-bar phrase. The EX-24 sampler was used, along with a custom sample library of sounds. The track was also sequenced from an M-Audio 88 keyboard controller. The hand drum (wooden djembe cajon) is a real-time overdub. I like to add real instruments over sequenced grooves at times to loosen them up and add that human time-feel, mixed in with the sequenced beat. Experiment with different increments of quantizing when you are sequencing your beats to find the right feel.

Track 70 is another groove sequenced in Logic. This four-bar phrase was created with the EX-24 sampler along with a custom sample library of sounds, and again sequenced from an M-Audio 88 keyboard controller. The brushes on the snare drum are a real-time overdub. When you are sequencing grooves, experiment with overdubbing a real instrument in real time, over the groove.

Additional Tips

- Mix it up: play some of the parts from a keyboard, and play some from a pad-to-MIDI controller.

- Experiment with different quantize percentages.

- Sequence a part in real time (i.e., hi-hat) over a part that is quantized (i.e., bass drum).

- Sometimes a mistake can lead to a great idea when you're sequencing.

- Whatever controller you're using to program or sequence, make it an extension of you.

- In the end, it's all about the groove.

SWING FEEL

A swing feel is a time-feel that is derived from triplets. To be able to play a swing time-feel, you must be able to acclimate to triplets. Jazz, blues, shuffles, and hip-hop all come from a triplet time-feel. The following exercise will help you to feel the triplets. The triplet is played with a right-hand lead. When the ride cymbal is added, the left-hand note on the middle beat of the triplet is played very lightly, as a ghost note.

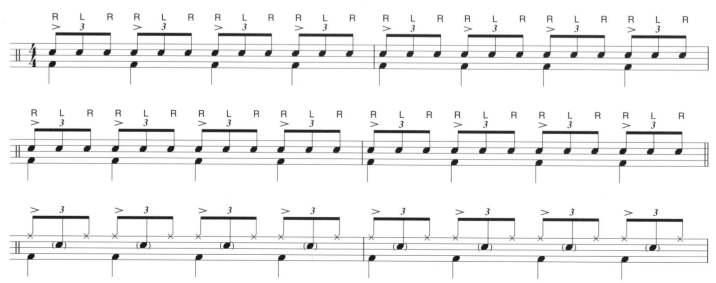

After you learn the above exercise, practice it at different tempos and change the phrasing length as well as the orchestration. For example, play phrases of eight or sixteen bars instead of four. After you practice this for a month, you'll notice that your swing feel, when playing triplet-based grooves, will swing more.

SAMBA

The samba is a popular Afro-Brazilian music and dance form. The Carnival celebrations in Rio de Janeiro gave the samba worldwide recognition. The samba groups are referred to as "Escolas de Samba" ("samba schools"). Each group chooses the theme for the decoration of the floats, costumes, dancers, marchers, music, and lyrics, and is judged on different categories. These are big productions including organizers, choreographers, dancers, costume designers, drummers, singers, painters, sculptors, and musicians.

Most samba groups are quite large and can have up to 5,000 members. The percussion section is called the "bateria" (which means "percussion section" or "drumset"), and can include anywhere from 300 to 500 percussionists.

The influence of Brazilian music is heard in jazz as well as contemporary music. Some musicians and groups influenced by Brazilian music include Stan Getz, Charlie Byrd, Chick Corea, and Santana.

Some of the traditional percussion instruments include different sized surdos, shakers, tamborims, agogo bells, cuica, snare drums, repinique, pandeiro, cymbals, triangle, and caxixi.

Samba is usually written in cut time (2/2), but you will also see it written in 2/4 and 4/4 (see example below) at times. It has a strong two-feel with an accent on beat two. This is usually played on the *surdo* (a large kettle-shaped drum). The surdo is the heartbeat of the ensemble. You can substitute a large floor tom for the surdo while playing the drum set.

The next example is a samba march feel, played on the drumset. The two-bar basic groove is written below, but **Track 72** goes a bit further. A shaker and tubano part are also included on the CD track. Notice that the ostinato bass drum phrase is based on a dotted-eighth–sixteenth-note rhythm.

TRACK 72

Getting your whole body to move in two is the key to playing the samba feel. You need to find your dance in this groove. Practice playing upbeat sixteenth notes and other syncopated rhythms against the samba bass drum. See *Over and Through the Bar Line* (p. 82), for more ideas on playing the samba feel. In addition, check out *World Beat Rhythms Series*: *Brazil* by Ed Roscetti and Maria Martinez (Hal Leonard).

SHUFFLE

The shuffle is one of the hardest grooves to play. In this triplet-based time-feel, it's very important to be able to play ghost notes off the triplet around the backbeat. Review *Swing Feel* (p. 106) for the triplet concept. It will help you with any shuffle feel in any style.

TRACK 73

Example A is a shuffle feel with a dotted-quarter–eighth-note ostinato in the bass drum. Listen to the lope of the hi-hat. This really bluesy shuffle is organized into a four-bar phrase.

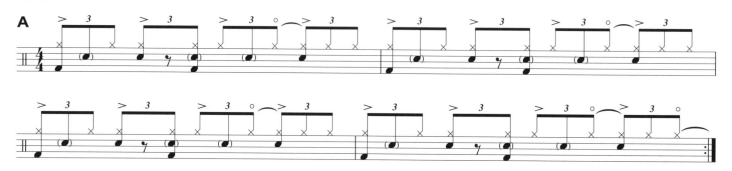

Examples B and C demonstrate a few other shuffle grooves. Example B is a jazz shuffle in the style of Steve Gadd, and C is a rock shuffle in the style of Jeff Porcaro. Play all unaccented snare drum notes as ghost notes.

Experiment with these shuffle grooves and some of your own over a twelve-bar blues form.

Remember to listen to a lot of blues music so you can start feeling the shuffle swing feel. For more information on this subject check out my book/CD *Blues Drumming* (Hal Leonard) and Jeff Porcaro's *Instructional DVD for Drums* (Hal Leonard).

SECOND LINE (NEW ORLEANS)

"Second line" is a drumming style of New Orleans, also known as the "traditional New Orleans funeral march." The clave rhythm is similar to the Bo Diddley beat. It involves marching (cadence-type) snare drum beats. A band made up of brass instruments and drums in a traditional New Orleans funeral ceremony would play somber cadences on the way to the cemetery with the mourners following just behind. The group of mourners became known as the "second line." These mourners would dance in the streets behind the band to release their sorrows. The rhythms played by the drums during this portion of the ceremony became known as "second line" rhythms or "street beats."

Zigaboo Modeliste and Johnny Vidacovich were among the first drummers to combine second line with syncopated funk grooves, creating a style that came to be known as "second-line funk drumming." Many famous bands from New Orleans (the Meters, for example) helped to popularize this style.

The next example shows this type of groove played on the drumset. It's all about the snare drum and the bass drum phrase. The first eight bars have been notated for this groove, which is organized into two-bar phrases. On the CD, the drumset part is improvised off the orginal two-bar phrase as the track plays out. The tambourine part was overdubbed.

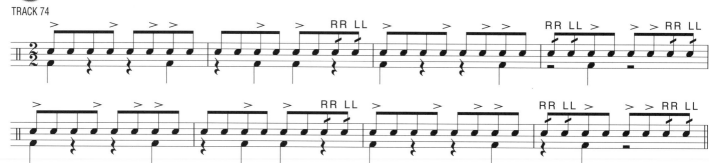

The bass drum is close to the Bo Diddley beat. Working on your rudiments, rolls, and marches will help you with this groove. Then you just have to stay loose and swing.

SUBBING

One way to get started in the business is to let other drummers know that you are available to sub for them if they need you. If another musician refers you for a job or you sub for the drummer, it's a great way to get heard by other musicians. The following tips will help you get started:

- Invite musicians to your gigs so that they can hear you play. No one is going to send you to sub for them if they don't know how you play.

- Be mindful that you're just filling in for someone—it's not your job.

- Be on time.

- Be prepared.

- Be patient.

- Show up with a good attitude.

- Remember to groove hard and play for the music. Don't overplay.

- Follow the charts and keep your place.

- Remember to get contact information from all the musicians you meet at the gig.

- Stay in touch with people—that's how you get referrals.

- Make sure you call the person for whom you subbed, thank him/her, and give a report on how things went on the job. Always follow up.

- When *you* need a sub, return the favor. Always take the time to help someone.

- Remember, once you can cut the job, this business is about three things: relationships, relationships, and relationships. Good luck!

SOLO

When you are soloing, you will either be playing alone or the band might be comping for you while you solo. If you are soloing alone, you should be playing over a song form or playing over a phrase. This way you can solo over the form, an ostinato, or riff in your head.

Example A shows the basic phrase structure for the solo break on **Track 75**, which is felt as 3/4–3/4–2/4 (as shown by the dotted bar lines), all within two bars of 4/4. This two-bar phrase happens eight times to make up the sixteen-bar form, shown in its entirety in Example B.

TRACK 75

Learn this solo, beginning at a slower tempo, and then write a solo break of your own. Try to make your solos as musical as possible. Your ideas should be influenced by the time-feel of the song. Don't force licks into your solo that don't belong, or that sound unmusical. Listen to the drummers that move you when they solo.

SYNCOPATION

A syncopation is a rhythm having the beats or accents displaced so that strong beats become weak, and vice versa.

Even-note Syncopation

The stress in non-syncopated rhythms occurs on the beat, as in Example A. Also, in meters with even numbers of beats (2/4, 4/4, etc.), the stress normally falls on the even-numbered beats. If the odd-numbered beats are stressed instead, the rhythm is syncopated.

Offbeat Syncopation

The stress can shift by less than a whole beat so that it falls on an offbeat, as in Example B, where the stress in the first bar is shifted by an eighth note.

Playing a note ever-so-slightly before or after a beat is another form of syncopation because this produces an unexpected accent.

Practice playing a groove that is syncopated with downbeats, going directly into a groove that is syncopated with upbeats, as in Example C.

TEMPO

Some Tempo Indications

A tempo: Return to the original speed.

Tempo giusto: In correct time: at a proper, appropriate pace.

Tempo ordinario: In the ordinary tempo for a given style.

Tempo Primo: In the first, or original time, after a passage has been in a different tempo.

Tempo rubato: Irregular time.

Being aware of and tuned in to the tempo of the song is an art in itself. Conditioning your body to feel different tempos in real time without a click takes time and patience. Work on different tempos with a click and then without. For example, say you are trying to feel ♩ = 120 bpm. After you play that tempo enough, it becomes easier to find without reference to a click. You can use a digital click with a flashing light to find song tempos if you're counting off the songs onstage.

Tempo changes are usually communicated to a group two ways: 1) they're conducted by the musical director (MD) or conductor; or 2) if you're using a click track with headphones (in the studio or live), a new tempo will be clicked out to introduce the tempo change.

TOM-TOM

The tom-tom is a cylindrical rod-tensioned drum with wooden shells, with heads stretched over the top and bottom part of the drum (although concert toms have heads on the batter side only). The tom-tom was originally used as a form of communication in Native American, Asian, and African cultures. In the early twentieth century, the toms (usually two or more) were added to the standard drum kit.

As modern tunable tom-toms were designed and became more widely distributed, the drums became mountable on stands with adjustable frames to change the height and angle. The woods generally used to make toms are maple and birch. Maple will produce a warmer tone while birch will project more. The amount of plies in the wood also affects the sound. The fewer plies the drum has, the more it will ring, while thicker plies create a darker sound.

TRACK 76

On **Track 76**, the two toms (12" and 16") are played with mallets against a quarter-note bass drum pulse.

When you are choosing toms for your set, you should base the sizes on the style of music that you will be playing. Larger toms are good for rock. Medium to smaller sizes are good for funk and jazz. Today, toms range in size from 8" to 18" in diameter with a variety of depths.

When you pick out your tom-toms, make sure you play them with the rest of your drumset so you can hear and feel how they blend together. Always use the sticks that you will be playing with in the style. Have someone else play the toms while you step back and listen. This way you can hear how they sound and blend with the drumset in the room.

Pacific LX and CX toms were used on the accompanying CD in the following sizes: 7" x 8", 8" x 10", 9" x 12", 12" x 14", and 14" x 16".

Rack toms

Floor toms

TAMBOURINE

TRACK 77

The tambourine is a percussion instrument resembling a shallow drum with metal discs (jingles) around the edge, played by shaking or hitting with the hand. In *Click Tracks* (p. 18), the importance of being able to overdub a shaker, the same is true for the tambourine. **Track 77** features an overdubbed sixteenth-note tambourine part over a second-line New Orleans groove played on the drumset. The tambourine was played by shaking it with two hands.

Tambourine

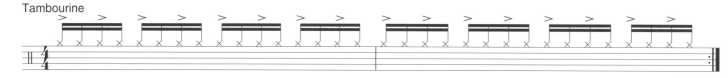

Practice playing tambourine parts to your favorite songs. Work on playing on beats 2 and 4 to match the snare backbeat. Listen to some old Motown and check out the classic tambourine parts. For suggestions, see *Motown* (p. 72) and listen to **Track 48**. Also come up with your own parts, and work on getting a good sound so that you can overdub tambourine in the studio and play it on a live gig.

TUNING

There are many approaches to tuning drums, but two major methods will be discussed here. The first is my approach to the conventional way of tuning. As usual, I like to keep it simple. The first thing is to start off with a drum that has a good shell, with good bearing edges. Put your top and bottom heads on loosely (if it's a tom). I like to put the bottom head on first. As you tighten the head, move across from one lug to the next, one full turn of the drum key at a time until you arrive at your desired tension and pitch. Tap the drum with a stick next to each lug, close to the rim, and listen to try to get each lug close to the same pitch. Repeat the same process with the top head. The top and bottom heads can be the same tightness and pitch, or one can be higher or lower than the other. It just depends on the sound you're looking for and how all your toms sound together as a whole.

Every drum has a sweet spot. I like to experiment with a drum until I find that spot and then tune it and leave it alone, making only minor adjustments. I use the same approach with my snare drums and bass drums, adding or taking away any dampening (small rings of duct tape for the snare, and foam or a pillow for the bass drum—unless you want it wide open). Then, if I or someone else wants a different sound, I change the drum rather than doing any drastic tuning from the sweet spot. That's my trick. I like to have drums set up and tuned for different styles of music. If I want a bigger and lower sound and pitch, I'll go with bigger drums.

The second approach is a new tuning technology that I've been using, developed by Drum Tech. It's called the DTS Tuning System. The DTS enables fast and easy drum tuning by eliminating the need to adjust tension rods. Tuning is now accomplished by adjusting the single DTS tension bolt. This "one-touch" approach allows you to listen to all aspects of the drum sound change while tuning. Most importantly, the top and bottom heads are now easily brought into tune with each other, producing the best overall drum sound. The DTS adds a completely new level of creative control in fast pitch adjustment for playing different styles of music with the same kit. You can also put a DTS on the bottom head of your toms only, and tune the top head the traditional way, with a drum key. I like this approach to tuning because it enables me to keep the bottom head more in tune, and then I can tune the top head the way I like, and easily de-tune one lug if I want to get a funky sound.

TRACK 78

Track 78 demonstrates using the tuning key on a tom-tom. Listen for the changes in pitch. I can raise or lower the pitch of the top head to the desired pitch while the drum is in tune with the bottom head.

Remember to experiment with different tunings for your drumset and choose a tuning combination that is right for both you and the style of music you are playing.

12" tom with DTS

TECHNIQUE

Whatever technique you decide to study and use on the drumset, it should assist and enable you to achieve your musical goal in any given performance. And under no circumstances should it interfere with your ability to groove. Your technique on the instrument gets you through the night when it's 110 degrees onstage and you're not feeling well. It also enables you to relax and play what you hear in your head.

There are many approaches to technique on the drums, and it would take at least a book this size to scratch the surface. So instead, I'll give you a list of tips to think about, and then you can find a good teacher, pick your poison, and dive into the technique(s) of your choice. Good luck!

- There are many grips; find one that is right for you.

- Stay relaxed—don't grip the stick too tightly.

- Don't push too hard at first. You don't want to hurt your wrists.

- Let the stick bounce up off the drum. Use and control gravity.

- Learn to play with your wrists, fingers, and arms.

- Experiment and find a bass drum and hi-hat technique that's right for you. Just because a specific technique works for someone else does not mean it's the right technique for you.

- Play all your technique exercises (including rudiments) very slowly at first. This will help your muscles to develop correctly.

- Be open-minded to new techniques and suggestions from your teachers and fellow drummers.

- Your technique should never get in the way of the most important aspect of drumming—the groove!

- If while playing you're thinking about your technique rather than the music, you are probably not groovin'.

TIME (TIME-FEEL)

Time is the rhythmic pattern or tempo of a piece of music. "Time" usually falls into one of two classes: *duple*, divisible by two; or *triple*, divisible by three. There is playing "in time" and there is playing "in time" with a "time-feel." The two are not the same. Do not get the two confused. You can be playing in time, but with no forward motion or lope in the groove. It would sound and be technically correct, but it would be as if you were standing still and not creating a forward groove.

Your time-feel defines who you are as a drummer. When you are playing in time with a strong time-feel in the style, you are in command of the situation. Where you put your time-feel in the groove of the song is your signature on the music. Being in touch with your emotions helps you to feel and find the right time-feel for the song. It's like acting—you have to get there emotionally, relive the groove in the style, find your dance, and create that forward motion. For more information on this subject, check out the following publications: *Drummer's Guide to Odd Meters* and *Funk & Hip-Hop Drumming* by Ed Roscetti (Hal Leonard), as well as *It's About Time* by Fred Dinkins (Warner Bros.).

UNIVERSAL LANGUAGE

Music is a universal language. You can be in many countries throughout the world and may not be able to speak the language; but pick up an instrument, and you can immediately communicate with people.

Once I had a student in an ensemble class from Beijing, China. He played bass and was one of the first music teachers given passage to leave China to come and study music in the United States. He did not speak any English, and when I first tried to communicate with him, we were getting nowhere. When it was his turn to play, I started to write everything down on paper for him in universal musical terms that he would know. For example, if I wanted him to play a repetitve pattern on the bass, I would point to the one- or two-bar bass line on the chart. The fact that he was able to read music enabled him immediately to understand, and we were able to communicate on a musical level to some degree. Over the weeks that followed, I was able to write down key musical phrases to help him get through the charts. The situation improved over time and he acclimated well to the ensemble. Our communication had improved without ever speaking a word.

Music is a universal language. We can learn from an experience like the one above and apply it to many situations in music and our lives in general. Sometimes less is more, even when we *do* understand each other.

VOLUME

Creating a balanced volume between your bass drum, snare, and hi-hat or ride is essential to your sound. Record yourself and listen back for the following:

- Make sure your grooves are not top heavy (too much snare and hi-hat, and not enough kick).

- Make sure your grooves are not bottom heavy (too much bass drum, and not enough snare and hi-hat).

- Make sure your grooves are not backbeat heavy (too much backbeat, and not enough kick and hi-hat).

- Once you achieve a balanced volume within the kit, work on maintaining that balance when changing your overall dynamic level on the drumset.

- When you are performing live, you will have to adjust your overall volume to fit the style of music you're playing. For example, if you're playing a concert in an arena, you will be playing louder than if you're playing a dinner set at a nightclub.

- If there are no microphones on your kit, you have to blend acoustically with the amps onstage. It's not always easy to do. Use your ears and have someone in the band walk around the room, listen to the band, then report back to you so you can make adjustments as needed. Do not let guitar or bass players place their amps behind your drumset. You never want amps shouting at you from the back of your head. Keep that space open for a monitor if needed.

VOCALIZE

To vocalize is to sing with the use of vowel sounds, instead of words. Vocalizing can be done in order to develop technique, tone, and rhythmic phrasing through the practicing of vocal exercises. There is an old saying, "If you can sing it, you can play it." Singing rhythms out loud will help you to stop counting rhythms when playing, and internalize them instead.

Practice singing rhythms from the guides that you wrote in *Rhythmic Guide* (p. 96). This is an exercise you can do either at or away from the drumset. Play sixteenth notes with an egg shaker in one hand, and play the upbeats of the sixteenth notes with your opposite hand on your hip. Tap your foot (right or left) to a quarter-note pulse. Sing a rhythm from your rhythmic guide out loud. Create your own vocal syllables for the rhythms. Play four bars of time (without singing) and then add your vocal for four bars. Repeat this exercise using different phrase lengths and tempos. Turn your rhythms into ostinato bass lines that you can sing as well. After you do this exercise for a month, you will notice a change in your ability to play rhythms. This technique will also help if you are a singing drummer in a band!

WORLD MUSIC

World music is music from the developing world, incorporating traditional and/or popular elements. By studying world music, you will be able to add elements of it to your own playing to create hybrid grooves.

The next example uses a hybrid African drumset. The groove is a 6/8 feel, notated in 4/4 time. The concept for this groove was to start out on the hybrid drumset and create an open and tonal 6/8-feeling groove and then overdub other hand drum tones, chants, bells, and whistles. Example A shows the basic groove. The drums are very tonal (definite-pitched) in this performance.

TRACK 79

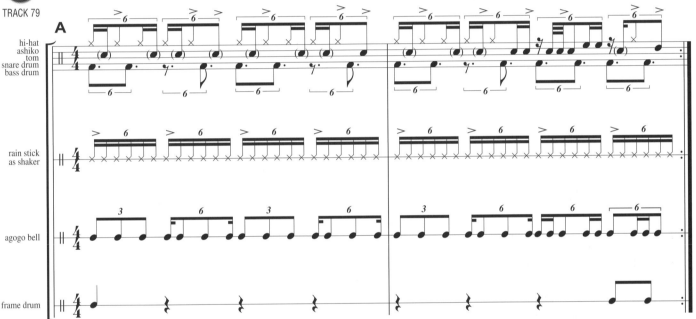

To create and record this example, the drumset was played first. The bass drum has a nice, wide open tone to it. It is an old vintage Slingerland 18" bass drum, with Fiberskyn 3 heads (Remo) on both sides, wide open with no muffling. The snare is a 10" popcorn snare (Pacific) with a Fiberskyn 3 head as well. The toms are Pacific LX Maple 10", 12", and 16" drums with Fiberskyn 3 heads. The cymbals are a Traditional 17" thin crash (Paiste), 16" fast crash, and 14" medium hi-hats. The ride cymbal is a 20" Dimensions dry ride, and the funky trashy cymbal is a Noiseworks Triple Raw Smash (Paiste). The second snare drum is an Ashiko 12". Thai sticks (Regal Tip) were used, and the groove was played to a quarter-note cowbell click.

The rainstick played as a shaker, was overdubbed next, followed by an agogo bell and frame drum (Remo). After that, a cajon bongo improvisation, a vocal chant track, and then finally a wooden whistle improvisation rounded out the recording.

The next example is a hybrid Olodum (Northeast Brazil) groove. The first parts to be recorded were bass drum, snare drum, and hi-hat, played with Blasticks (Regal Tip). The next part is an overdub of two tom-toms played with mallets (Regal Tip). A 16" floor tom was then recorded, played like a *surdo*, using a mallet. (The surdo is a Brazilian kettle-shaped drum that is the heartbeat of the ensemble.) The shaker sound is a rainstick played like a shaker.

TRACK 80

The improvised percussion part is a 10" popcorn snare with the snares turned off, played like a timbale with thin timbale sticks (Regal Tip). Example B shows the basic groove.

The drumset used for this example was a maple Pacific CX kit: 22" bass; 12", 14", and 16" toms; a 14" bronze snare drum; a 10" popcorn snare; and 5000 Series pedals (DW). Cymbals included Traditional Series (Paiste) 20" ride, 16" and 18" crashes, and 14" hi-hat. Remo Ambassador heads were used on the top and Diplomat on the bottom. Power Stroke 3 (Remo) heads were used on the back bass drum head, and a clear Ambassador head on the front head with a hole cut in the center and a pillow placed inside the drum.

If you wish to simulate some world music beats, experiment with setting up different hybrid drumsets of your own. Think outside the box and consider the drumset as an overdub instrument, with traditional and non-traditional world percussion instruments added to the mix.

WALTZ

The waltz is a musical style in triple time (3/4) that gave rise to an accompanying dance of rhythmic twirls, which included bending and rising in a circular formation around the dance floor. This grew to be the most popular ballroom dance of the nineteenth century. The word "waltz" is derived from the Latin verb "volvere," meaning to rotate or turn.

Origins of the waltz can be hard to define, and the process was gradual that defined the waltz as a separate dance that accompanied this musical style. As a dance, it was popularized in Vienna in the latter half of the eighteenth century, to be embraced and developed further by many nineteenth- and early-twentieth-century composers. The waltz paved the way for other ballroom dances and inspired many jazz artists to cover songs in waltz time, as well as to compose new tunes using the 3/4 time signature.

A jazz waltz is a composition played by jazz musicians in a syncopated 3/4 or 6/8 time signature. A jazz waltz has a strong swing feel.

Notable Jazz Waltzes

The following were either composed as jazz waltzes, or are frequently played as such:

- "All Blues" (Miles Davis)
- "Gary's Notebook" and "Boy, What a Night!" (both from *The Sidewinder* by Lee Morgan)

- "My Favorite Things" (associated with John Coltrane)
- "Some Day My Prince Will Come" (associated with Miles Davis)
- "Waltz for Debby" (Bill Evans)
- "West Coast Blues" (Wes Montgomery)
- "Wild Flower" (Wayne Shorter)

Example A is a jazz waltz swing feel in four-bar phrases. **Track 81** features an extended version of the basic waltz notated below. After you have learned these first eight bars, transcribe the rest of the four-bar phrases from the CD and practice them at different tempos.

TRACK 81

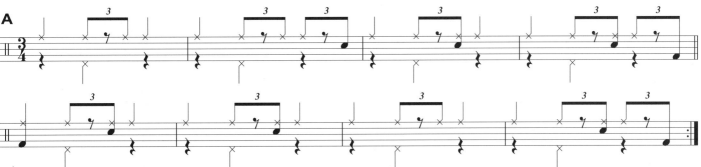

Example B is a four-bar phrase. It consists of two bars of time going into two bars of right-hand lead with triplets. During the basic groove, feel free to improvise on the snare drum and bass drum.

Examples C–J are in 6/8 time. These will give you a few additional ideas of how to play in a jazz waltz swing feel. For more information on this subject, check out my book/CD *Drummer's Guide to Odd Meters* (Hal Leonard).

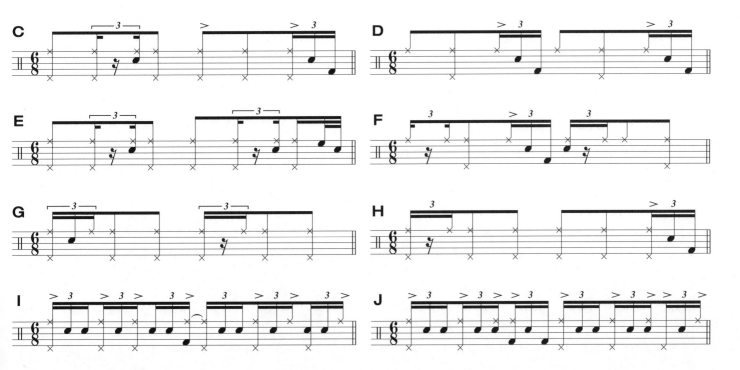

X-RAY

X-ray your playing! Record yourself when practicing or playing at a rehearsal or gig. At a later date, listen back to analyze and critique yourself. You can also have your drum teacher listen and ask him/her to analyze and critique you. This is a good habit to develop. You will discover things about your playing that are good, as well as identify any bad habits right away and be able to work on correcting them. You can also videotape yourself. This will enable you to see your body language at the drumset, as well as to hear yourself. By x-raying your playing, you will improve at a faster pace.

YIELD

There you are, playing the coolest groove of your life. You're in the zone and it never felt better. Then all of the sudden someone in the band says to you, "Hey! You're stepping on the melody!"

You should always yield to the melody. Knowing the song form and where you are in the tune is not enough. You must know the phrasing of the melody. Whether it's an instrumental melody or vocal melody doesn't matter at first. The important issue is to know the phrasing so that you do not step all over the melody with your groove and fills. This should be your first thought when learning a new song. Play a simple groove and listen to how the melody is phrased, and the sound of the voice or instrument playing the melody. After listening to and learning the melody, you will have a better awareness of what the song needs from you.

The same thing goes when you're playing with a rhythm section. Play simply at first and listen to the other instruments in the section. Lock in with the bass and strive to play together as a unit. Come up with parts that make the band groove and the melody shine.

ZOOM

The next example is a warm-up exercise that I have used over the years to increase speed in both hands. This exercise will also help you to lead with your left hand. Start at a tempo with which you are comfortable, and play each example for two minutes, stopping in between examples. Increase your speed one bpm every other day until you reach your desired tempo. It's more about your accuracy than your speed, at least at first.

ZANY GROOVES AND FILLS

I'd like to end the CD with a favorite 4/4 funk groove. It is a two-bar phrase that may be felt instead as three measures: 3/4, 3/4, 2/4. Examples A–D show four variations on the basic beat.

TRACK 82

124

Example E shows the basic rhythm of one possible fill idea. Though it is notated for snare drum, you may apply the rhythm around the kit. This fill goes over the bar line. In the 2/4 bar at the end of the phrase, the "free beats" indication means that you can play whatever you want in the last two beats. It will be like a 2/4 turnaround back to the beginning of the phrase.

E Fill idea

In closing, I wish you much happiness in your life pursuits and behind the kit. Remember to keep groovin'.

All the best,

Ed Roscetti

You can correspond with Ed Roscetti at his website at **www.roscettimusic.com** and at **www. worldbeatrhythms.com**. Find out what he's up to in his studio and see when he will be in your neighborhood conducting a clinic, music camp, or concert soon.

HAL•LEONARD DRUM PLAY-ALONG™

Play your favorite songs quickly and easily with the *Drum Play-Along*™ series. Just follow the drum notation, listen to the CD to hear how the drums should sound, then play along using the separate backing tracks. The lyrics are also included for quick reference. The audio CD is playable on any CD player. For PC and Mac computer users, the CD is enhanced so you can adjust the recording to any tempo without changing the pitch!

Book/CD Packs

VOLUME 1 – POP/ROCK
Hurts So Good • Message in a Bottle • No Reply at All • Owner of a Lonely Heart • Peg • Rosanna • Separate Ways (Worlds Apart) • Swingtown.
00699742   Book/CD Pack $12.95

VOLUME 2 – CLASSIC ROCK
Barracuda • Come Together • Mississippi Queen • Radar Love • Space Truckin' • Walk This Way • White Room • Won't Get Fooled Again.
00699741   Book/CD Pack $12.95

VOLUME 3 – HARD ROCK
Bark at the Moon • Detroit Rock City • Living After Midnight • Panama • Rock You like a Hurricane • Run to the Hills • Smoke on the Water • War Pigs (Interpolating Luke's Wall).
00699743   Book/CD Pack $12.95

VOLUME 4 – MODERN ROCK
Chop Suey! • Duality • Here to Stay • Judith • Nice to Know You • Nookie • One Step Closer • Whatever.
00699744   Book/CD Pack $12.95

VOLUME 5 – FUNK
Cissy Strut • Cold Sweat, Part 1 • Fight the Power, Part 1 • Flashlight • Pick Up the Pieces • Shining Star • Soul Vaccination • Superstition.
00699745   Book/CD Pack $12.95

Prices, contents and availability subject to change without notice and may vary outside the US.